FAMILY MATTERS

FAMILY MATTERS

A Bible Study on Marriage and Family

MICHAELANN AND CURTIS MARTIN

EMMAUS
ROAD
PUBLISHING

A division of Catholics United for the Faith
Steubenville, Ohio

Emmaus Road Publishing
827 North Fourth Street
Steubenville, Ohio 43952

Library of Congress Control Number: 2002090788
ISBN 1-931018-14-6

On the cover
The Martin Family

Cover design and layout by
Beth Hart

Nihil Obstat: William C. Beckman, M.T.S., *Censor Deputatus*
March 22, 2002
Imprimatur: ✠ Charles J. Chaput, O.F.M. Cap., D.D., Archbishop of Denver
April 5, 2002

To Our Lord Jesus Christ, for the truth He gives us in His teachings and the power of His grace that He gives us in the sacraments.

To our parents, Don and Frances Dudley and Brock and Carole Martin, whose love and example have been the foundation of our marriage.

To our children, Brock, Thomas, Augustine, MariAnna, Philip, and Joshua, with whom we have the joy of following Jesus Christ.

Contents

Contents

Abbreviations

Old Testament
Gen./Genesis
Ex./Exodus
Lev./Leviticus
Num./Numbers
Deut./Deuteronomy
Josh./Joshua
Judg./Judges
Ruth/Ruth
1 Sam./1 Samuel
2 Sam./2 Samuel
1 Kings/1 Kings
2 Kings/2 Kings
1 Chron./1 Chronicles
2 Chron./2 Chronicles
Ezra/Ezra
Neh./Nehemiah
Tob./Tobit
Jud./Judith
Esther/Esther
Job/Job
Ps./Psalms
Prov./Proverbs
Eccles./Ecclesiastes
Song/Song of Solomon
Wis./Wisdom
Sir./Sirach (Ecclesiasticus)
Is./Isaiah
Jer./Jeremiah
Lam./Lamentations

Bar./Baruch
Ezek./Ezekiel
Dan./Daniel
Hos./Hosea
Joel/Joel
Amos/Amos
Obad./Obadiah
Jon./Jonah
Mic./Micah
Nahum/Nahum
Hab./Habakkuk
Zeph./Zephaniah
Hag./Haggai
Zech./Zechariah
Mal./Malachi
1 Mac./1 Maccabees
2 Mac./2 Maccabees

New Testament
Mt./Matthew
Mk./Mark
Lk./Luke
Jn./John
Acts/Acts of the Apostles
Rom./Romans
1 Cor./1 Corinthians
2 Cor./2 Corinthians
Gal./Galatians
Eph./Ephesians
Phil./Philippians

Abbreviations

Col./Colossians	Jas./James
1 Thess./1 Thessalonians	1 Pet./1 Peter
2 Thess./2 Thessalonians	2 Pet./2 Peter
1 Tim./1 Timothy	1 Jn./1 John
2 Tim./2 Timothy	2 Jn./2 John
Tit./Titus	3 Jn./3 John
Philem./Philemon	Jude/Jude
Heb./Hebrews	Rev./Revelation (Apocalypse)

Chapter 1

Building on the Rock

E very week, people get married in the United States. Each couple hopes to find joy, happiness, and love in their marriage. They stand with sincerity before their family and friends. Many of the marriages even take place in churches, so the bride and groom are also standing before God to profess their love. So why do so many marriages struggle or fail? These aren't bad people. What's wrong with these marriages? Where do we turn to find the support and assistance we need to make our marriages work? Is there something missing in marriage today? Is there any hope?

Just a Thought

Imagine a man and a woman who love each other very much. One day they decide to build their dream home. Each of them is very eager to begin this project. They look forward to sharing their lives together in their new home. They go down to their local home improvement store and buy all sorts of building materials and tools. Then they go to their perfectly selected spot and, side by side, begin hammering boards together in an attempt to build this dream home. But something is missing.

No amount of love, sincerity, enthusiasm, or dedication can ever make this house a reality without a blueprint or detailed plan. Similarly, no amount of love, sincerity, enthusiasm, or devotion can make your marriage a lasting success without a blueprint. Jesus Christ has given a blueprint for marital happiness to the Catholic Church. In this study, we want to explore the teachings of Jesus Christ and discover the keys for building a marriage and family on a foundation of solid rock (cf. Mt. 7:24-25).

Where to Start

Imagine a fleet of ships on a journey to a distant destination. C. S. Lewis asserted that three things are necessary for the fleet to succeed. First, each ship must be seaworthy and functioning properly. Second, the ships must avoid crashing into one another. Finally, the captains must know where the entire fleet is going. If any of these components is missing, no amount of hard work or good intentions will save the fleet from disaster.[1]

Marriage is like this fleet of ships. If we want to succeed, we must first have our own life in working order. Then we must take care to avoid crashing into one another through selfishness or a lack of thoughtfulness. Finally, we must know where our marriage and family should be headed, so that if we fall off course, we can make the necessary changes to come back on course.

The very best place to start is at the beginning. We need to ask ourselves, "What does God want from us?" More than anything, He wants us to know, love, and serve Him in this life and then be with Him in heaven for all of eternity. The best way to get to know God is to spend time with Him in prayer, receive His life-changing power through the sacraments, and read His words to us in Sacred Scripture. After we begin to get to know God, we will find ourselves falling more and more in love with Him. The amazing thing about love is that it moves us to do things for the loved one. The same is true with God. When we really love Him, we are drawn to seek and to serve Him in our thoughts, words, and deeds.

Why is this important? It's important because all people, whether we are single or married, are looking for love. We are looking to other people to give us good feelings of self-worth and affirmation. As much as we may want to find that perfect someone to fulfill all of our hopes and dreams, the fact is that we are all broken and fail to meet each other's expectations. The only

---

[1] C. S. Lewis, *Mere Christianity* (San Francisco: Harper, 2001), 69 ff.

person who will be able to satisfy us completely is Jesus Christ. That's why it is important to be in right relationship with God and to learn what He wants for each of us. Then and only then will we discover His overwhelming peace and joy in our lives. If we have this priority in place, then we will be equipped and prepared for the relationship that God has designed for each of us.

Once we seek and accept God's mercy and forgiveness, we are able to get our spiritual life right with God. Then we will be ready to work on making a marriage all that God wants it and has designed it to be.

Throughout this Bible study, we will develop these concepts and examine the three necessary elements of a successful, loving marriage:

1. Faithfulness, the total gift of self by one spouse to the other; in other words, no adultery
2. Indissolubility, the lifelong nature of marriage; in other words, no divorce
3. Fruitfulness, the openness to children; in other words, no contraception

These three elements encompass God's goals for each of us in marriage. He wants us to be faithful to our spouse for our entire life and be open to His blessings in children. We will discuss the biblical basis of these elements as well as the timeless teachings of the holy Catholic Church.

In the Beginning

The place to start is with you and your relationship with Jesus Christ. It may seem odd that a Bible study on marital relationships begins by focusing on an entirely different relationship, but as C. S. Lewis said, each ship needs to be watertight and seaworthy in order to survive the journey. What type of marriage will we have if one or both spouses are not living according to God's blueprint for their lives? What kind of marriage might we have if we can't avoid crashing into one another and hurting one another's feelings? How can we live in harmony and seek fulfillment with our spouse if we don't have a personal sense of what we want out of life? What is our final destination?

The answers to these questions lie in God's plan for each individual. He created each one of us and has blessed us with guidelines for avoiding disaster and reaching our God-made goals. Are we willing to trust Him to form us for the sake of our marriage? We may be surprised to find out that we will be greatly blessed, and so will our marriage!

In the beginning was the Word, and the Word was made flesh (cf. Jn. 1:1,14). Jesus is the Word, and He became flesh in order to save us and offer us eternal life with the Father, Son, and Holy Spirit. It is only fitting, then, that we begin our study with the Word, Christ Himself. How can we have Jesus Christ at the center of our personal lives and at the heart of our marriage? Where can we turn for answers? Where and when do we get started on this adventure? Let's go straight to God's love letters to us—the Gospels, and the rest of Sacred Scripture.

Personal Application

1. God's plan leads us to happiness. Read the following verses and fill in what God is promising each of us.

a. Jeremiah 29:11

_____

_____

b. John 10:10

_____

_____

2. What keeps us from experiencing the happiness of God's plan for us? What answers are found in the following passages?

a. Isaiah 53:6

_____

_____

b. Romans 7:15-25

_____

_____

> *Man, tempted by the devil, let his trust in his Creator die in his heart and, abusing his freedom, disobeyed God's command. This is what man's first sin consisted of. All subsequent sin would be disobedience toward God and lack of trust in his goodness.*
> *—Catechism, no. 397*

3. Jesus provides us with truth and grace—His very life and power—to overcome sin and be reunited with God and His loving plan. What are we told in the following verses? What is the role of Jesus in bringing us back to God?

a. John 14:6

_____

_____

b. John 3:16

_____

_____

_____

4. We must accept Jesus as the Lord of our lives.

a. Read Matthew 7:24-27. What is the only difference between the two men?

_____

_____

b. Read Luke 6:46-49. What does Jesus expect from us?

_____

_____

c. Read Acts 2:38. What does Saint Peter tell us to do?

_____

_____

_____

To repent means to change our life, our actions, and our thoughts. According to the Catechism (no. 397), sin is caused by disobedience and a lack of trust; therefore, repentance entails placing our trust in God and obeying. Baptism is the introduction into the sacramental life of the Church. Through each of the sacraments, Christ gives us His life and power to imitate Him. Without Jesus and the sacraments, our good intentions and repentance would not be enough. Saint Peter teaches us in Acts 2 that we need both the desire to change (repentance) and the power to change (which comes from Jesus through the sacraments).

5. Reunited to God, we are brought back into God's family, the Catholic Church. With the teachings of the Church and the sacraments, our individual and family lives can reflect the love of Christ.

a. Read Ezekiel 36:25-28. What does the prophet say will happen when we are sprinkled with the waters of Baptism in the New Covenant?

_____

_____

_____

b. Read Acts 2:42. To which four things do the disciples of Jesus devote themselves?

(1)_____

(2)_____

(3)_____

(4)_____

In this study, we will explore the teachings of the apostles, but there is more that you must be prepared to do. Seeking out committed Catholic friends (fellowship), leading a sacramental life with the Eucharist and Confession (the breaking of the bread), and praying are the essential actions that the wise man must do in order to succeed in life and in marriage.

Talk Tips

This section of the Bible study is designed to aid couples in communicating their thoughts and ideas to one another after completing the study questions.

- Is Jesus the center of your life? If not, are you willing to make Him number one?
- What resolutions or steps are you going to take in order to get to know Christ better?
- On a scale of one to ten, how would you rate your marriage?
- How can you build on the rock of Christ in your marriage?

Action Points

- Decide how you can specifically make Christ the Lord of your life. Have you made a good Confession recently?
- How can you show your spouse that you are willing to make Christ the center of your relationship?
- Make a monthly date to work through this study.

Chapter 2
Together in Prayer

I s Jesus Christ really the key to a successful marriage? Yes, because Jesus provides the only protection against marriage's deadly enemy, and only He can give us the one thing we need to make our marriages work.

As the Catechism explains, marriage was designed by God to succeed. Marriage still works, if we can overcome the devastating effects of sin, which can lead us to stumble and fail in loving our spouses for life:

> According to faith the disorder we notice so painfully does not stem from the *nature* of man and woman, nor from the nature of their relations, but from *sin*. . . . To heal the wounds of sin, man and woman need the help of the grace that God in his infinite mercy never refuses them. Without his help man and woman cannot achieve the union of their lives for which God created them "in the beginning" (Catechism, nos. 1607-8, original emphasis).

The true enemy of marriage is sin, and Jesus Christ has conquered sin. Sin has damaged our nature so that we are not able to love the way we would want to. The one thing we need for our marriages to succeed is God's grace, which allows us to give and receive true love. The grace of God heals our brokenness, restores our ability to love, and allows us to become sons and daughters of God who are capable of sharing in His own divine life. With God's grace, we can develop a willingness to care for others even when it hurts. Jesus not only overcomes sin, but He shares His very life with us so that we may imitate Him.

By coming to restore the original order of creation disturbed by sin, he [Jesus] himself gives the strength and grace to live marriage in the new dimension of the Reign of God. It is by following Christ, renouncing themselves, and taking up their crosses that spouses will be able to "receive" the original meaning of marriage and live it with the help of Christ. This grace of Christian marriage is a fruit of Christ's cross, the source of all Christian life (Catechism, no. 1615).

Christ is the source of this grace (Catechism, no. 1642, original emphasis).

In the last chapter, we looked at God's invitation to each of us to make a commitment to Christ. We saw the importance of looking to Christ as our Lord and Savior. Following Christ is both a decision and a daily process. Once we personally accept Christ, it is necessary to go further and make Him the Lord and center of our marriage relationship.

Curtis and I (Michaelann) had the great fortune of meeting at a Catholic Bible study that Curtis was leading. Both of us had fallen away from our faith during college, and after our conversions we really valued our Catholic faith. Our experience of falling in love as active Catholics helped us to see the importance of having a Christ-centered relationship. We both experienced the dynamic impact of the truth of Christ, the life-transforming power of the sacraments, and the vital importance of committed Christian friends. Because of these beginnings, it has been easier to remember that our marriage and family need to remain centered on Christ and His Church. There have been times when the distractions of family life make prayer very challenging, but we continue to strive to make it a priority.

Living a Life of Prayer

When Michaelann and I were newlyweds, all we wanted to do was be together. We went together to the grocery store, and Michaelann even came to my basketball games. We visited friends and family together and just about everything we did, we did together. This time of togetherness was great. The key was learning how to harness our love for each other and directing it toward Christ and others. We knew that if we gave ourselves to Christ, He would bless us and become the wellspring of our mutual love. With Christ at the center of our lives, our love for each other would increase and begin to overflow to others.

There was one thing that we had to do alone. We couldn't very well go into the confessional together. When I (Michaelann) was in Confession one Saturday afternoon, it dawned on me that many of my closest relationships were suffering because of a lack of individual attention on my part. As I was talking with this wonderful priest, he reminded me that it was great to be in love and spend time with my spouse but that when we each die, we will stand alone before God. He basically told me that I needed to get back to my private prayer time as well as continue to nurture my prayer life with Curtis. We can only be our best together if each of us is personally seeking Christ. What a challenge this has been, yet the wisdom of this advice has been a great blessing to our marriage.

Listen to the beautiful words of the early Christian Tertullian, as quoted in the Catechism:

> How can I ever express the happiness of a marriage joined by the Church, strengthened by an offering, sealed by a blessing, announced by angels, and ratified by the Father? . . . How wonderful the bond between two believers, now one in hope, one in desire, one in discipline, one in the same service! They are both children of one Father and servants of the same Master, undivided in spirit and flesh, truly two in one flesh. Where the flesh is one, one also is the spirit (Catechism, no. 1642).

Single life and married life are very different, particularly after the children arrive. I (Curtis) remember actually having quiet time with God in prayer. It is unusual now to spend time reading the Scriptures or going to daily Mass without a few distractions.

Family life requires balance. How do we keep our priorities in order when there seems to be limited time? The whole honeymoon experience has the potential to shift the emphasis from living a life centered on Christ to living a life centered on each other. In fact it is interesting to note that the traditional meaning of the word honeymoon was literally the time it took for one sweet moon to pass, one month, indicating that the time after marriage is typically very sweet and might be very brief before children arrive. We are convinced that most couples experience adjustments in priorities in this regard. Now we feel like old married folks, since we can spot newlyweds a mile away. What a gift that early devotion toward one another is.

We shall share some insights from the Scriptures and the Church's teachings on the value of striving to keep Christ at the center of our lives, marriages, and families and just how we are supposed to be able to do this.

Prayer with Your Spouse

The Couple to Couple League (CCL) stresses the importance of not only intimate communication with your spouse but also the great importance of praying together. *Creative Abstinence*, a little pamphlet published by CCL, encourages couples to pray together:

> We find that when we spend time in prayer, especially prayer together, morning and evening, our lives go smoothly. . . . When we, as a married couple, spiritually join together in prayer we can experience a spiritual wholeness that is just as satisfying in its own way as the physical joining of husband and wife. This is a gift, or grace, of marriage. When we accept and use this gift, we can find a new, dynamic, and rewarding facet of our life together with each other and with God.[1]

This pamphlet is very encouraging and helpful in strengthening communication between spouses. We will address in greater

---

[1] Oscar and Susan Staudt, *Creative Abstinence* (Cincinnati, Couple to Couple League, 1999), 4.

detail responsible parenthood and the use of natural family planning in a future chapter.

Prayer in the Family

If you have children, you may wish to consider designating a special time to praying as a family. As I (Curtis) have been working with the college students involved in the Fellowship of Catholic University Students (FOCUS) program, I have come across some insights about the importance of family prayer. We have been blessed to meet exceptional young people throughout the country. When I meet college students who are exceptionally committed to their faith and excited about evangelization, I ask them questions about their childhood and faith formation. There is a common thread that connects almost all of these exceptional young people: All of them remember their family praying together. For some, it was kneeling around the parents' bed for night prayers; for others, it was reciting the Rosary as a family, or a profound awareness of their parents' faith, as manifested in family participation in the sacraments and family prayer time.

Each family has to find out what will work best for its individual situation, but the proof is in these faithful young people. There is power when a family prays together.

Personal Application

1. Read Matthew 14:23, Matthew 26:36-44, Mark 1:35, and Mark 6:46. What was an essential part of Jesus' life?

_____

2. Consider that Jesus was God and yet He still spent time in prayer. How then are we called to imitate Christ in our daily lives?

_____

_____

_____

> *Those who pray are certainly saved;*
> *those who do not are certainly damned.*
> *—Saint Alphonsus Liguori*[2]

3. How are we supposed to fit prayer into our busy schedule? It's as easy as one, two, three!

a. One: What to do? Read Matthew 6:33-34.

_____

_____

b. Two: How to do it? Read Romans 12:2.

_____

_____

c. Three: How to live? Read Philippians 4:4-6 and Romans 8:28.

_____

_____

_____

4. Does prayer apply to our marriages? Read Tobit 8:4-8. What do Tobias and Sarah do together?

_____

_____

5. Read Ecclesiastes 4:12.

a. What is the image given in this verse?

_____

_____

---

[2] *Del gran mezzo della preghiera*, in Catechism, no. 2744.

b. Are we willing to try to establish that cord that cannot be easily broken? How can we do so?

_____

_____

c. What are the strands of the threefold cord?
   (1)_____
   (2)_____
   (3)_____

6. Scripture teaches us about the importance of family prayer.

a. Read Matthew 18:19-20. What does Jesus promise to those who pray together?

_____

_____

_____

b. Read Acts 1:14. What is happening in this verse? Who are the people mentioned? What is their relationship to Christ?

_____

_____

c. If we are called to follow Christ and His teachings, should we not also take these actions and make them a part of our own family life? How can our families more fully devote themselves to prayer?

_____

_____

In the first chapter, we noted the importance of following Christ by living out the actions listed in Acts 2:42. We are called to a great responsibility as parents to model these actions to our children and live our faith to our greatest ability. We need to remember that devoting ourselves to the apostles' teachings, fellowship, the breaking of bread, and prayer are the foundation stones of our faith as well as our marriage.

Talk Tips

- Now that you've completed the application questions, do you see any gaps in the framework of your own marriage? If so, what might you do in order to find greater unity in your life as a Catholic Christian and as a married couple striving for success?
- What might you be able to do as a couple in order to transform your minds and hearts together? Completing this study together is a great starting point.
- Are you nervous about, or do you feel awkward about, praying aloud with your spouse? Are you willing to pray with your spouse, despite your nervousness or awkwardness, for the sake of your marriage?
- Is there a good time for you to pray together daily as a couple?
- If you don't have a prayer time for the entire family, what might be the best time to set aside?

Action Points

- Decide together at what time you will pray daily as a couple and as a family. Do your best to hold each other accountable to your resolutions.
- It may be difficult to pray aloud with your spouse if you don't have the habit established, but we encourage you to make the effort to be vulnerable with each other in the presence of God. He will bless you for your efforts and shower you with the grace you need to succeed. Make the effort to make God the center of your marriage and your family.

Chapter 3
Spelling Love Takes T-I-M-E!

Michaelann and I have fond memories of our time of courtship: living an hour apart, calling each other at spontaneous moments, and asking the other to meet at the midway point, Denny's. We used to race each other to see who could get there first, as if this were a proof of our love. In fact, we developed a growing commitment to each other through our willingness to meet and spend time together.

Then there were those dates that were made with meticulous details and arrangements all in order before the big night. One date in particular, Curtis planned a beautiful dinner at a restaurant on the beach. He researched the time of sundown perfectly so that we wouldn't miss the beautiful sunset. It still stands out as one of the most memorable evenings we have spent together. Sure, it was easier back then to arrange a date or to meet at the drop of a hat because we didn't have a family, and all we wanted to do was spend time together. Now it is more of a challenge to make our time together special and meaningful. Recently, we have realized that even our definition of being alone has changed. Now, we consider ourselves alone if there is no one over three feet tall with us.

We have learned that it is so important to keep our marriage alive and well. Just as we feed our souls with prayer and our bodies with food, we need to feed our marriage. The type of food is what's different. We had a very good friend tell us that the best way to spell love is t-i-m-e. Think about it for a moment. All we have on this earth is time to live, and when our time runs out, we die.

Our society even goes so far as to say that "time is money," and people value money quite a bit.

In reality, time is more precious than money, because we can always get more money. Therefore, people must rightly value time. Don't we feel important when someone we know takes time off work or specific duties to do something kind for us or visit us? Or think about the many children who long for more of their parents' time—time to listen to the little things that happened throughout the day, time to laugh about the funny things, time to read a story and cuddle before bed. Time is our hottest commodity. How do we spend it?

> As if you could kill time without injuring eternity.
> —Henry David Thoreau [1]

Her Time, His Time

If we profess our love for our spouse, then it is our duty to show that love in how we spend our time. I (Michaelann) am a firm believer in the statement that "words are cheap." If they are not expressed through acts of love and kindness, then what value do they really have? That is why it is so important that Curtis's actions show me that his love is true and sincere.

Just as we show God how important He is to us by continuing to try to pray each day, we must show each other our love by giving our time. I spend my entire day surrounded by six children. I rarely get out, and when I do it is a wild day of errands, loading and unloading children at each stop. By the time Curtis gets home, I am usually in great need of his loving attention, adult conversation, and a firm embrace from *him*. There have even been those times when I have wanted to hand him the baby and run out the door, but by the grace of God we have been given wise counsel on how to deal better with the stress and business of family life and marriage.

---

[1] *Walden and Other Writings* (New York: The Modern Library, 1937, 1950), 7.

I (Curtis), on the other hand, drive home trying to forget about the hassles and financial struggles of my work and the many phone and e-mail messages and responses that I didn't get to that day. I try to adjust to the overflow of affection I will receive as I walk through the door and enter "Daddy mode."

Men and Women Are Different

This is where the challenge is for me as a man. Modern sociologists have studied our patterns of communication. They have found that the average man speaks about ten thousand words a day. The average woman speaks approximately twenty thousand! Here's my problem as a husband. I have gotten most of the talking out of my system by the time I come home; for Michaelann, it's halftime. I've learned that on my way home I need to undergo a transformation of thought. I am tempted to say, "I'm done, I'm ready to relax now." What I need to be thinking is "Now that my professional work day is finished, I can get to the really important part of my life." Once I realize that what I do from nine to five is secondary, then I can allow God to begin to sanctify my home life.

My first step is to connect with Michaelann. The very existence of our family is a physical manifestation of our fruitful love. So, too, I must be with Michaelann so that our love can overflow to our children. Even though I don't always *feel* the need to talk about our day, I do have that need. What the Scriptures tell us about our wives is a timeless truth: "It is not good that the man should be alone" (Gen. 2:18). By making myself available to Michaelann, I give God the opportunity to expand my heart. I made a number of rookie mistakes early on, and I still have to fight the temptation to solve the many "problems" Michaelann shares with me. I'm beginning to learn that she doesn't want solutions—she wants me. As I listen, I begin to allow her to draw me into the family's day. I learn where she and each of the children are. One may need encouragement; another, discipline. They always need my attention.

The Key in Communication

After several years of marriage, Curtis and I (Michaelann) found ourselves just living through each day and not embracing life with the zeal we once had. When we read some great books on the importance of communication in marriage, it changed our lives. We were challenged to talk about our feelings, thoughts, and hopes, and to discuss our common goals. It has been so great!

We have been encouraged to take the first fifteen minutes when Curtis arrives home to catch up on how each of us spent the day. The children know that this is our special time to talk and that we will be finished shortly. This makes the transition to family time very smooth and relaxing. We have also been encouraged to schedule thirty to forty-five minutes, one night a week, to talk about the budget, the children's needs, household problems, and other potentially stressful topics. These two steps—the daily discussion and the weekly "family maintenance" meeting—have allowed us to clear the static that creeps into family life. Then we would try to get out at least every other week for a date without the children. After implementing these simple tips into our family routine, we began to experience a second honeymoon in our marriage. We remembered how much fun we had together, we were better parents to our children, and we began to have better attitudes about the ups and downs of family life, all because we were willing to manage our time in such a way that we knew by our actions how important and loved we are.

I (Curtis) have to admit that the idea of setting aside thirty to forty-five minutes to talk about the hassles of family life wasn't an initial hit with me. In fact, it was the last thing I wanted to do. I was already frustrated. Our early dating had been fun. I like to have fun. After a few years of marriage, it seemed as if our dates had gone from fun to frustrating. We spent most of our time talking about challenges with the kids, difficulties with our finances, and home repair. Now I was supposed to dedicate one night a week to this stuff, too?

To my great surprise, something wonderful happened. We spent the thirty to forty-five minutes discussing our family's struggles and deciding how we could begin to tackle some of them. The next week, when we prepared to go out for some coffee, there she was, the woman I fell in love with. Michaelann was back! By taking some time to deal with the problems that had been burdening her, Michaelann was now freed up to enjoy our time together. Even if another problem was on the horizon, she knew that we could talk about it during next week's troubleshooting session. I had never understood how the normal hassles of life had been burdening my wife. Once I gave her the opportunity to share her concerns with me, she was freed up to have some fun.

Personal Application

Let's see how the Scriptures reinforce the bonds of love and friendship.

1. Read Malachi 2:13-16 and 1 Peter 3:7-9. In what ways does a man honor his wife?

_____

_____

_____

2. The Book of Proverbs is filled with God's words of wisdom. Read Proverbs 5:18-19.

a. What is the challenge for the wife?

_____

_____

b. What is the challenge for the husband?

_____

3. Note how Scripture powerfully expresses the desire of lovers to spend time together. Read Song of Solomon 2:8-10 and 5:16.

a. How might we apply these verses to our own marriage?

_____

_____

b. How might we free our spouse to be able to come away with us?

_____

_____

4. Let's return to the Book of Proverbs for some timeless advice. According to Proverbs 17:17, do friends turn love on and off at their own convenience?

_____

5. Read Proverbs 18:19. What is quarreling likened to in this passage?

_____

_____

6. Read Ephesians 4:26. How important is talking things out? How and when should we work out our difficulties?

_____

_____

7. Read Proverbs 25:11. How are we instructed in this passage to communicate with others?

_____

8. Read Proverbs 31:10-12, 26. This chapter of Proverbs could be the basis of an entire Bible study for wives. Here, we wish to consider the great blessing of a good wife.

a. What kind of woman is she?

_____

_____

b. What does verse 26 tell us about her?

_____

_____

9. Proverbs 20:5 tells us something about the man who is willing to take time to explain himself. How is he described?

_____

_____

10. Read Ephesians 4:15-16 and 5:15-16 for some final words of encouragement. How are we to speak to our spouses?

_____

_____

Talk Tips

- Now that you have had an opportunity to read God's Word about living in greater harmony with your spouse, what might you do to strengthen your relationship?
- Share with each other your memories from your favorite date. What made it so memorable? What was the most enjoyable moment?

Action Points

- Schedule thirty or forty-five minutes to discuss the challenges currently confronting your marriage. Once you have discussed the challenges and come up with a plan for the future, plan a time to enjoy each other's company.

This initial troubleshooting session may seem a bit overwhelming, but it is vitally important to clear away any static in your relationship in order to rediscover the joy of loving each other. Love isn't always easy, but it's always worth it!

Chapter 4
As Christ Loves the Church

Why is it so difficult for men and women to embrace the Church's teaching on marital love? Our society often rejects these teachings as old fashioned and out of date. Others are frightened by the vulnerability they call for. In these days, after all, can we trust God and our spouse enough truly to love without thought of ourselves?

These teachings of the Church come into a new light when we understand and embrace our own masculinity and femininity. Adam and Eve were created "in God's image and likeness" (cf. Gen. 1:26-27). Eve was to be a suitable partner, and the two were to complement each other. We need to realize that men and women are wonderfully different by design, yet equal in dignity and honor as sons and daughters of God.

The most challenging passage in Sacred Scripture concerning the complementarity and radical interdependence of husband and wife is Ephesians 5:21-24:

> Be subject to one another out of reverence for Christ. Wives, be subject to your husbands, as to the Lord. For the husband is the head of the wife as Christ is the head of the church, his body, and is himself its Savior. As the church is subject to Christ, so let wives also be subject in everything to their husbands.

To many, this passage seems very outdated or even barbaric. At the very least, many argue that it has little to do with modern culture and family life. But the Scriptures continue:

Husbands, love your wives, as Christ loved the church and gave himself up for her, that he might sanctify her, having cleansed her by the washing of water with the word, that he might present the church to himself in splendor, without spot or wrinkle or any such thing, that she might be holy and without blemish. Even so husbands should love their wives as their own bodies. He who loves his wife loves himself. For no man ever hates his own flesh, but nourishes and cherishes it, as Christ does the church, because we are members of his body (Eph. 5:25-30).

The call for wives to submit to their husbands is challenging, but we must remember the teaching's context: Marriage is to reflect the love of Christ and the Church. Submission means literally to order one's mission to another's. The wife's mission is to follow her husband's leadership as he lays his life down for her and for their children. Pope John Paul II stresses the importance of an authentically Christ-centered vision of marriage by pointing to the sacrifice of Jesus for His Bride, the Church.

In this sacrifice there is entirely revealed that plan which God has imprinted on the humanity of man and woman since their creation; the marriage of baptized persons thus becomes a real symbol of that new and eternal covenant sanctioned in the blood of Christ.[1]

As Christians, we are subject to Christ, yet we do not lose our dignity. Rather, our dignity is infinitely greater because we are children of God. So, too, a wife's submission to her husband ought to allow her husband to grant her honor through his Christlike love and concern.

The Church has given us practical wisdom for discovering God's plan of blessings for us on this earth and then in heaven. As Jesus puts it, "I came that they may have life, and have it

---

[1] Apostolic Exhortation on the Role of the Christian Family in the Modern World *Familiaris Consortio* (November 22, 1981), no. 13.

abundantly" (Jn. 10:10). Yet Satan tricks us, as he did Eve and Adam, into mistrusting God, our loving Father. We must realize that we can trust our heavenly Father because He really does have our best interests in mind when He offers us solutions for living joyful, holy marriages. It is a constant struggle to fight the Devil as he continuously works to undermine our trust in God (cf. Catechism, no. 397).

Once we realize that the Devil's basic temptation is to get us to mistrust God, it's easier to see that we should work to trust Him and fight the temptations. This is particularly true when it comes to the Church's teaching on masculinity and femininity. We need to trust in God's plan.

Holy Headship

Before we were married, we had the great fortune of spending many hours together talking about what we thought our marriage and family should be like. We talked about our hopes and dreams, our ideas about raising children, and everything we could think of that related to marriage and family life. As we talked, both Curtis and I (Michaelann) realized that we shared the conviction that a mother staying at home to raise the children was the most noble and vital role a woman could have in the family and in the world.

These conversations were great while we were dating. After we got married, some of our shared views became a bit more challenging. We had moved to Ohio to allow Curtis to attend graduate school. Originally, we were both going to attend, but with the birth of our first son—and the news that our second son was on the way—our plans changed. I told people that I was postponing graduate school for a semester or so and left it at that. I found actually staying home more of a sacrifice than I had expected. I am so grateful that I had more than just feelings to base my decision upon.

It wasn't long after the move before we realized that being married and having a family were challenging emotionally and financially. The graduate school years were very lean. Curtis had always said that if we went without a meal or any necessity, he would take that as an indication from God that he needed to quit school and return to full-time work to provide for the family. I approved of that in theory but, again, following it in practice was another ballgame. Tuition and the cost of living were driving us into poverty, and I spent most of my day in our one-bedroom garage apartment feeling helpless and unproductive. Living out these convictions became a daily struggle.

Still, I was able to see time and time again that God desired me to stay at home and raise Brock, even when opportunities to work outside the home might have been possible.

Needless to say, we have had our fair share of "Ephesians 5 experiences" where I honestly have had to trust in Curtis's leadership of our family. Recently, when we found out that our son, Philip, was autistic, we were reminded of how differently we respond to life's obstacles. We found that for the most part, Michaelann (and most women) are more emotional and relational than the men in their lives; hence, it makes sense that women are called to be the heart of the home. We were also reminded of the greatness of God's design for hierarchy in the family.

We learned that Philip was going to need much more of our time and attention, and this was going to cause some significant changes in our family life. As I considered these changes, I realized that I had become very emotionally invested in staying at home and homeschooling our children. I knew I wanted what was best for our children, but my pride had clouded my good judgment for a brief time. I had family and friends suggest putting our older boys in school so that we could get a handle on Philip's care and treatment, but I didn't budge. Then I had doctors present the same suggestion, as well as a priest in spiritual direction. At that point, I discussed the matter with Curtis, and he decided that we should at least look into it. I had to restrain my pride, admit I couldn't do it all, and submit voluntarily to his leadership.

I felt as if it would take a miracle to change my mind. We had investigated the schools and thought that the best option for us was a local Christian school. Unfortunately, there was a long waiting list for every grade. This all happened during Christmas break. When I called the school, there happened to be two openings occurring at mid-semester break. The openings "just happened to be" in the grades of our two eldest sons. If that weren't enough of a sign from God, the admissions director chased after us in the parking lot to explain that our tuition would be reduced significantly because Curtis worked full time in campus ministry. God not only opened up the space but also took care of the costs! By accepting Curtis's leadership, I was able to let go and let God bless us. It was difficult to admit my weakness, but God continues to show us how wonderfully the family works when we follow His plan.

We like to think of this as just another "Ephesians 5 experience." Curtis was willing to sacrifice for our family, and I was having a difficult time with pride. When I realized what God was allowing us to experience, I was able to submit to Curtis's leadership and recommit myself to motherhood with a sense of joy and happiness, knowing that this was God's will for us. God continues to provide for our needs and take care of everything. All we have to do is live with an openness to His plan and try to live it out faithfully.

I am so thankful that Curtis has been willing to lay down his life for me and for the family as Christ did for the Church. It has made submitting to his leadership so much easier. It has not been a relationship of an overlord and a servant, as the world would like us to believe, but more akin to a partnership of head and heart working together for the common good of the body. If a body had an impaired brain, it would be unable to function properly. If a body had an impaired heart, the body's lifeline would be threatened. Both head and heart are essential to the body's proper functioning. Without one or the other, the body could only continue to exist by extraordinary means. When both the heart and the head work together, there is health; when they don't, there is disease, or even death. God made us to complement each other, and when we do, things work out well. It all hinges on trusting in our loving Father's plan and being willing to follow that plan, even when the Devil and the world are whispering seeds of doubt into our ears.

We have a great role model in the Holy Family. Saint Joseph was called to care for and protect Mary, his wife, and Jesus, the Son of God. There may have been times when Joseph would have liked to have stayed home to be with Mary and Jesus, but he followed God's plan for husbands and made sure their needs were met. His sacrifices were countless, as were Mary's. And think of it: Joseph was called to be the head of the Holy Family, even though Jesus was God and Mary had been preserved from original sin.

In *Casti Connubii*, Pope Pius XI describes beautifully how marriage and family life imitate the Trinity in life-giving love. He further explains our masculinity and femininity in light of our married roles. Just as men, through their masculinity, take primacy in the order of leadership, women through their femininity take primacy in the order of love.[2]

Holy Heart

Just as we can look to Saint Joseph as the head of the Holy Family, we can look to Mary as our greatest example of femininity in the family. I had a friend ask me why there was so little in the Bible about Mary and women in general. I was intrigued by her questions and also her indignant claim that women are always going to be second to men as a punishment for original sin. After some thought and prayer, I was able to discuss Mary with her.

---

[2] Pope Pius XI, Encyclical on Christian Marriage *Casti Connubii* (December 31, 1930), no. 27.

In Mary, we have a woman conceived without sin, a woman perfect in every way. She was called to be the Mother of Jesus, the Son of God, and she spent her life at home being a wife to Saint Joseph and raising Jesus in poverty and simplicity. She could have done anything—she was beautiful, intelligent, and perfect—and she chose to serve God in this way. She lived in complete humility and submission to His plan. She embraced the ups and downs, the great joys and sorrows that came with being the Mother of Jesus. After a life of loving faithfulness, she was rewarded by being assumed into heaven and honored as the Queen of heaven and earth, first in honor among all of God's creation. She is our greatest role model and support.

When things get difficult, when being a wife and mother don't seem to be enough, and there aren't many affirmations for jobs well done, we can go to Our Lady and gain strength from her example of love through service. In her life, we learn that through embracing humility and simplicity we will best serve God and remain united to Him in heaven for all eternity. This world is not our true home, and we don't want to get too comfortable here, or else we may not long for God and our true home, heaven.

So it is with our marriages. When we work together as God designed, our day-to-day activities will go more smoothly than if we try to function on our own.

Personal Application

1. Trusting in our heavenly Father, read Genesis 3:1-4. Notice how the serpent tries to get Eve to doubt the goodness of God's command. How was Satan tempting Eve? Isn't it ironic that Adam and Eve were already "like" God, but Satan still was able to plant seeds of mistrust and doubt about His fatherly care?

_____

_____

2. Read Catechism, no. 397.

a. In what ways does our modern culture tempt us not to trust God?

_____

_____

b. How do we trust in God as a Father who will love and care for our every need?

_____

_____

c. Do we trust that He has good reasons for creating men and women equal in dignity, but very different from one another?

_____

d. How can we trust God by living our lives as either masculine or feminine, as He designed us?

_____

_____

3. Read Ephesians 5:21-32. Realize that Ephesus was one of the most anti-family cultures of the ancient world. Ephesus was the home of the Temple of Artemis (Diana), one of the seven wonders of the ancient world and a center for cult prostitution. Saint Paul's teaching that each spouse is called to serve the other was as countercultural then as it is now.

a. How does Christ ultimately serve His Bride, the Church?

_____

_____

b. What do husbands need to be willing to do for their wives in imitation of Christ?

_____

_____

c. How are wives called to love their husbands, just as the Church submits to Christ's authority?

_____

_____

4. Read Mark 10:42-45.

a. Why did Jesus come to us?

_____

_____

b. If we are to imitate Him, what are we called to do?

_____

_____

5. Jesus, as always, is our example. Read John 13:12-17. What is Jesus teaching us?

_____

_____

_____

6. Read Psalm 100:2. What is the attitude that we need to have when serving God by serving others?

_____

_____

Talk Tips

- In Ephesians 5, Saint Paul teaches about the restoration of God's original order in the family. He does not justify male domination, but calls husbands to love their wives as Christ loves the Church. The counterpart of this call is a wife's "submission" to her husband. This means allowing her husband to love her this way, that is, allowing her husband to serve her as Christ serves the Church. Wives must also love their husbands in return as the Church loves Christ. What do you think about this wonderful call to serve in marriage?

- Do you (men) recall an experience in which you were challenged to make a tough decision for the family, and your wife supported you? Do you (women) recall a situation in which following your husband's lead was difficult, but you did so out of a desire to love and honor him? Share those memories, and discuss how they have strengthened your marriage.

- Discuss any fears you may have about abandoning your marriage and family totally into God's hands. There is great strength in being vulnerable with your spouse and growing through difficulties together.

Action Points

- If your roles as husband-father and wife-mother are not yet clearly defined, try to take some time and talk about what you think God is calling you to in your marriage.

- After talking about changes to improve how you live out your masculinity and femininity, commit to making positive changes, and hold one another accountable to your goals.

- Make an effort to affirm your spouse when you notice that he is trying to live out his goals.

- Celebrate your marriage by going out on a date together.

Chapter 5
Sacred Sex

Does the Church really say that sex isn't good? Yes. Christianity has clearly taught for two thousand years that sex isn't good. It's much more than good—it's sacred. It's ridiculous to think that God is opposed to sex; He created it. God could have made us like amoebas, so that we'd simply go along, and when we were ready we'd simply split into two. Or He could have made us like most fish, where the female deposits her eggs and the male comes by later and fertilizes them. This was not God's design, and if we want to live our marriages with an abundance of life, then we'll need to see that in marital love, love-giving and life-giving are intimately united.

The Church is not against sex; she is against the misuse of sex. Why? Because as the Mystical Body of Christ, the Church possesses a deep insight into how important intimacy truly is. If we abuse intimacy, we not only make a mockery of our love for one another, but also sin against ourselves and turn our backs on our loving Father (cf. 1 Cor. 6:18-20).

How could something that feels so good outside of marriage be so bad and cause so much damage? Sexual intimacy outside of marriage is a counterfeit. It looks like real love and intimacy, but it is a lie. The Devil highlights the God-designed pleasure and togetherness and then tricks us into choosing the side effects without fully choosing the goodness.

The FBI

One of the responsibilities of FBI agents is to detect and confiscate counterfeit money. Agents undergo the best possible training, so that no matter what type of counterfeit money they encounter, they will always be able to detect it. Providing such training could seem almost overwhelming. There are countless forms of counterfeiting, and counterfeiters are always coming up with new tricks. Yet during their training, the FBI agents do not even look at a single counterfeit. They simply focus all of their efforts on studying the real thing (cf. Phil. 4:8), so that when a counterfeit presents itself, they will know immediately it is a fake.

When it comes to marital intimacy, what is the real thing? Marital love is designed to be a celebration of the love between the spouses. Within sacramental marriage, there is a lifelong, exclusive relationship which allows the lovers to give of themselves freely and without reserve. God has so designed marital love that these times of intimacy flow from the couple's mutual love and increase their love as they share themselves with each other. This love is so real and so powerful that it is the very life source of the family, a life source that is so tangible that it may take the form of a new human life. The foundation of this love is the lifelong bond of fidelity and trust between the wife and husband. Pope John Paul II expresses this truth very beautifully:

> Every man and every woman fully realizes himself or herself through the sincere gift of self. For spouses, the moment of conjugal union constitutes a very particular expression of this. It is then that a man and woman, in the "truth" of their masculinity and femininity, become a mutual gift to each other. All married life is a gift; but this becomes most evident when the spouses, in giving themselves to each other in love, bring about that encounter which makes them "one flesh" (Genesis 2:24).[1]

---

[1] Letter to Families *Gratissimam Sane* (February 2, 1994), no. 12.

God's plan is designed with our true happiness in mind. We have found that intimacy plays a great role in maintaining our unity, emotional stability, and peace in marriage, and in keeping us sensitive to and enamored with each other, in good times and rough times. Marital union is an earthly icon of the intimacy God desires to have with us. We are made to give and to receive love, because we have been created in His image:

> God is love and in himself he lives a mystery of personal loving communion. Creating the human race in his own image . . . God inscribed in the humanity of man and woman the *vocation*, and thus the capacity and responsibility, *of love* and communion" (Catechism, no. 2331, original emphasis).

Giving It All Away

What does it mean to be made in God's image? Let's take a few moments to understand this image better. God is a communion of Persons: Father, Son, and Holy Spirit. The Father's love is infinite; from all eternity He gives of Himself perfectly and completely and He never ceases to give all that He is. This gift is so real that it *is* the Son, who is literally "God from God . . . true God from true God, begotten not made, one in being with the Father" (Nicene Creed). The Son is the perfect reflection of the Father, and so He also gives all that He has, and this infinite, mutual self-gift of the Father and the Son is so real that it is the Holy Spirit, the living bond of love between the Father and the Son. Each Person loves perfectly and is loved completely. The image of our God is all about loving and self-giving. Because we are made in this image, we will find our greatest joy and happiness only in living in imitation of God's self-giving love.

Our self-donation takes its form as an offering of our body as a gift to our spouse. In previous chapters, we discussed serving each other in our positions within the family. Marital intimacy is a beautifully profound, God-given way to give ourselves totally to our spouse.

Our good friend Christopher West, former Director of the Office of Marriage and Family Life of the Archdiocese of Denver, offers some great insights into our Holy Father's teachings on marriage and family. He believes that the Sacrament of Marriage consists in the manifesting of the eternal mystery of God in a sign that serves not only to proclaim that mystery, but also to accomplish it in us. The sign is marital intercourse. He further explains that sexual intercourse is where the words of the wedding vows become flesh. Through the marital embrace, the bodies of husband and wife speak the language of God's total, faithful, fruitful love. West is simply echoing the words of Pope John Paul II:

> As ministers of a sacrament which is constituted by consent and perfected by conjugal union, man and woman are called to express that mysterious "language" of their bodies in all the truth which is proper to it. By means of gestures and reactions, by means of the whole dynamism, reciprocally conditioned, of tension and enjoyment—whose direct source is the body in its masculinity and its femininity, the body in its action and interaction—by means of all this, man, the person, "speaks." . . . Precisely on the level of this "language of the body"—which is something more than mere sexual reaction and which, as authentic language of the persons, is subject to the demands of truth, that is, to objective moral norms—man and woman reciprocally express themselves in the fullest and most profound way possible to them by the very corporeal dimension of masculinity and femininity.[2]

The challenge that we are given in marriage is living the gift of sacramental sex. The challenge in marriage is for husband and wife to love each other with the love of Christ. This means that in sexual union we are called to be a living and efficacious sign of God's love, and we must guard ourselves against thoughts and behaviors that are opposed to God's love. Anything that contradicts the free, total, faithful, and fruitful self-giving of the spouses is a violation of the meaning of authentic sexual intercourse.

---

[2] General Audience (August 22, 1984), no. 4.

Personal Application

1. We know that we are made in the image of God and that we are made to give ourselves to others in marriage. Our sexuality is holy.

a. What does Genesis 2:21-25 tell us about Adam and Eve before the Fall?

_____

_____

b. What is God's first command to Adam and Eve in Genesis 1:28?

_____

_____

We are also made to be attractive to one another. Read Song of Solomon 7:6-13 for a beautiful image of love and desire.

Now let's examine the Scriptures that support our total, faithful, and fruitful gift of love. There are instructions for both men and women. Let's take a few moments first to see what advice men are given in the Bible.

2. Read Proverbs 5:15-23, which provides us with an image that is appropriate to men in marriage.

a. What does this passage describe?

_____

_____

b. What does it mean?

_____

_____

3. Read Song of Solomon 4:4-16.

a. What is described?

_____

_____

b. Who or what is the man's garden and fountain?

_____

c. What is the duty of the wife?

_____

_____

4. What are husbands instructed to do in Ecclesiastes 9:9?

_____

_____

5. What do the passages we have just read seem to be telling us about the total, faithful gift given to our wives in marriage?

_____

_____

6. Read Hebrews 13:4. Notice the language concerning the marriage bed. What can we do to ensure that marriage is held in honor?

_____

_____

7. There are other challenges that are addressed specifically to women. We are called to offer our bodies sacrificially in bearing children, and also to train our daughters, granddaughters, and young women to live their femininity to the fullest. What counsel is provided in Titus 2:4 and Song of Solomon 2:7?

_____

_____

_____

8. Read together the beautiful love poetry in Song of Solomon 2:8-17, while keeping in mind that spouses' desires for each other are holy and good.

a. What are the love and desire between spouses compared to?

_____

_____

b. Does this passage instill in you a desire to be a better gift of love to your spouse?

_____

_____

Talk Tips

- Read together Song of Solomon 2:8-17 again and 5:1-12, 16. Doesn't reading these passages instill a greater desire for a more complete intimacy with your spouse?
- Might it be the time to rekindle the love of your youth?
- Talk to your spouse about how you can express your appreciation for each other more effectively.
- If you want a renewed romance with your spouse, tell him or her.

Action Points

- Take some time to talk about how, within your budget and means, you might be able to rekindle the love of your youth. Plan something fun and commit to doing it, as soon as possible!
- Think of ideas for a date, an evening alone, or even a weekend getaway.

Chapter 6

Openness to Life Equals Openness to God's Blessings

Michaelann and I have been blessed with six wonderful children. It's amazing how a large family can attract attention in today's world. A frequent challenge is the grocery store. The kids really do very well, but it's still a sight to see Mom and her little ducklings trailing behind with a shopping cart or two. Michaelann is frequently asked, "Are those all yours?" Questions like this tend to catch you off guard. Your mind is racing to think of a life-affirming response. One of our friends shared a good idea. She has eight children, and when the question arises, she gives a big smile and says, "Yes! We're Catholic," and then after a brief pause, "and we are trying to take over." This usually leaves the inquirer a bit confused. "Is she serious?" Well, in a way she is.

Unholy War

One of the most dramatic changes in our culture has been the shift from an attitude that has viewed children as a blessing to one that views them as a burden. Fertility is now considered a disease. This month alone 10,410,000 American women will take medication (the birth control pill) to "cure" them of fertility. Another 10,727,000 American women of childbearing age and 4,224,000 of their husbands or partners have surgically mutilated their bodies to render themselves sterile. In all, 64 percent of women who could become pregnant use some form of contraception.[1]

The more things change, the more they stay the same. Ours is not the first culture to declare war on our children. In fact, the diabolical temptation for parents to abandon and even destroy their children is a recurring theme in human history. David Chilton notes:

> From the first book of the Bible to the last, this is the basic warfare of history. The Dragon is at war with the Woman and her Seed, primarily Jesus Christ. . . . The most striking example of this pattern on a large scale occurs throughout the history of Israel, from the Exodus to the Exile: the covenant people's perennial, consistent temptation to murder their own children (Lev. 18:21; 2 Kings 16:3; 2 Chron. 28:3; Ps. 106:37-38, Ez. 16:20).[2]

The reason so many people fear children is that the Evil One has shifted our focus from the blessing of children to their cost. Yes, children are expensive—financially, emotionally, and physically. Whatever you have, your children are going to want it, and want it to a degree that will challenge your limits of generosity. Children will cause you to suffer. As Christians, we don't deny these facts; we simply view them in light of the fullness of truth. Children are a blessing from God. The only way to evaluate whether children are worth the cost is to ponder their value. When spouses come together in marital intimacy, there is a possibility that our loving God may bless that union with a new life. This child will be created in the image of God, and he will be called to live forever with Him in eternal blessedness. Once we realize this, we understand that their value infinitely outweighs their cost.

---

[1] Alan Guttmacher Institute, *Facts in Brief: Contraceptive Use* (2000), http://www.agi-usa.org/pubs/fb_contr_use.html.
[2] David Chilton, *The Days of Vengeance: An Exposition of the Book of Revelation* (Tyler, Tex.: Dominion Press, 1987), 307-8.

God's Plan for Families

The key to fostering a truly pro-life attitude is to keep our minds focused on the goodness of God's plan for our lives (cf. Jer. 29:11). Our heavenly Father has given us a blueprint for happiness in our married life; we need look no further than the very first commandment He gave us: "Be fruitful and multiply" (Gen. 1:28). Our modern world seems to have forgotten that the unselfish love of Christ is the pathway to everlasting happiness. For most of us, this pathway leads through marriage and parenting.

As parents, we can see the wisdom of the Almighty's plan. What, or who, can teach us heroic generosity better than children can? Children have a profound and positive influence on their parents. We have found ourselves doing things for our children that we never would have dreamed of doing for anyone else, and we even find joy in doing them!

At the heart of Christ's teachings about openness to life is the most central teaching in all of Christianity. In Scripture, just before we are told to "be fruitful and multiply" (Gen. 1:28), we are informed that we have been made in the image and likeness of God (cf. Gen. 1:26). This is a profound truth. God is, in His very essence, a community of life and love, and He has made each of us to be like Him and to be with Him. "God in His deepest mystery is not a solitude, but a family, since He has in Himself fatherhood, sonship, and the essence of the family, which is love."[3] So it is true that "God is love" (1 Jn. 4:8). We were made by this love, and we are made for this love. Marriage is designed by God to be a living image of His love. Husband and wife are to love each other and hold nothing back. Their love is so real and powerful that with God's blessing they may end up changing its diapers.

Contraception flies in the face of this beautiful teaching. Right in the depths of marital love, contraception says, "No!" Instead of

---

[3] Pope John Paul II, Homily at Mass for the People of Puebla de los Angeles (January 28, 1979), in *Puebla: A Pilgrimage of Faith* (Boston: Daughters of St. Paul, 1979), 86.

a total self-gift, the spouses begin to withhold themselves from one another. "I love you" is changed into "I love what you do for me, or how you make me feel, but I don't love you, at least not your maternity or paternity." But that's who we are. That's what marital intimacy is about. God has designed marital intimacy so that the love-giving and life-giving aspects cannot be separated without doing violence to our very selves. Often couples may have to accept that the blessing of children may not be given, but that's a far cry from intervening by way of drugs, chemicals, or some other action to render our lovemaking sterile intentionally.

Sterile Legacy

Unfortunately, the world's fear of children has crept into many people within the Church. We know many couples whose parents have lost the faith and have counseled their own children to use birth control, offering any number of excuses. Unfortunately, it is rare to find parents of the baby boomer generation who actually encourage their now adult children to be open to having children.

So what's the answer? Through Baptism, we became children of God. Our loving Father has provided a wonderful owner's manual for His children. It is called the Holy Bible, and it is fully understood within the rich teachings of the holy Catholic Church. Many popes and early Church Fathers knew that we, a weak, broken people, would need encouragement and guidance. They have written beautiful documents, sermons, and letters just so Christians could have a well-lit path to follow. This path ultimately leads to heaven, but begins with the road to holiness in this life. We hope these documents will shed light on your worldview so that we all might better understand the awesome call to parenthood found in the Sacrament of Marriage. We may want to note that never in the Scriptures is having children mentioned as a liability or punishment.

Before we continue, we must also add that the Church has always understood that there may be serious reasons why a couple should postpone having children. If a couple is undergoing physical, emotional, or financial difficulties, it's possible to use the natural rhythms of a woman's cycle to avoid a pregnancy. The Couple to Couple League does a wonderful job of explaining natural family planning (NFP) and distinguishing the radical difference between this form of responsible parenting and contraception.

Contraception is defined as the choice by any means to impede the procreative potential of a given act of intercourse. If spouses choose to engage in intercourse and in addition choose to do something else to make sure that specific act of intercourse does not result in a new life, then the spouses are contracepting—in other words, they are intentionally sterilizing their acts of intercourse. Christopher West sums up the problem with contraception:

> [T]o the degree that we knowingly and intentionally reserve any part of ourselves from our spouse in the sexual act, we cannot speak of a *total* self-giving. This includes our fertility. Contracepted intercourse contradicts the "language of love" by saying "I give you all of myself *except* my fertility. I receive all that you are *except* your fertility." The choice to withhold one's fertility during intercourse, or to refuse to receive it as a gift in one's spouse, is a contradiction of the deepest essence of conjugal love right at the moment when it should find its most sincere expression. Precisely at marriage's "moment of truth," the truth is exchanged for a lie.[4]

This brings us back to NFP. The reason that NFP is an acceptable method of regulating births, when there is a legitimate reason for doing so, is that it is in no way contraceptive— it in no way acts against God's plan for bringing life into the world. NFP is an effective and scientific method of regulating births or achieving pregnancy that involves first determining when a couple is likely to become pregnant (if they were to

---

[4] *Good News about Sex and Marriage: Answers to Your Honest Questions about Catholic Teaching* (Ann Arbor, Mich.: Servant Publications, 2000), 108.

engage in marital union) and then choosing either to engage or to abstain from intercourse at that time. Never do the spouses choose to impede the procreative potential of a given act of intercourse; never do they contracept. At the time when pregnancy is most likely to occur, there simply is no intercourse.

With NFP, the spouses are called to consider prayerfully being open to receiving new life. Being responsible entails being generous and only abstaining from intercourse when there is a just reason for doing so. NFP enables the couple to act in complete accord with God's design instead of acting against it by using some method of contraception. With NFP, a couple need never withhold anything of themselves from each other when they do engage in intercourse, and thus the spouses are able to respect the full truth of mutual self-giving:

> For just reasons, spouses may wish to space the births of their children. It is their duty to make certain that their desire is not motivated by selfishness but is in conformity with the generosity appropriate to responsible parenthood. . . . [Their behavior must] respect the total meaning of mutual self-giving and human procreation in the context of true love; this is possible only if the virtue of married chastity is practiced with sincerity of heart (Catechism, no. 2368).

Personal Application

1. In Psalm 127:3-5, we are given the image of a warrior with a quiver full of arrows.

a. What does this image teach us about children?

_____

_____

b. Who is the warrior?

_____

c. In which wars are we engaged?

_____

_____

2. In Psalm 128:1-4, we read about the image of an olive plant and many little shoots.

a. What does fear of the Lord mean?

_____

_____

b. What does it mean to walk in God's ways?

_____

_____

c. How does this relate to being open to children?

_____

_____

_____

d. Are children a blessing?

_____

e. Do we trust in our heavenly Father? To what extent?

_____

_____

_____

3. Read Genesis 15:2-6 and Genesis 30:1-2, 22-24.

a. What do these stories teach us?

_____

b. In these stories, is the parents' suffering great or light?

_____

_____

Read Catechism, no. 2374, and reflect upon the Church's deep compassion for couples who cannot have children.

4. Now let's look at some success stories with children. In Ruth 4:13-17, we read about Ruth's conceiving.

a. Who was the one in control of giving her a son?

_____

b. Who was Obed's grandson? Wouldn't it have been a great shame if Ruth didn't want children and rejected being open to them to the point of not allowing the Israelites to have this grandson?

_____

_____

_____

5. Consider the great example of Hannah in 1 Samuel 1:1-20. Her story has captivated the hearts of many women.

a. Who was in control of her fertility?

_____

b. Did she acknowledge God's omnipotence? How?

_____

_____

c. What did she do to show her faith and humility?

_____

_____

d. How was she rewarded for her faith and patience?

_____

e. What was her promise to God? Did she keep it?

_____

_____

6. Continue to read the rest of 1 Samuel 1-2. In 1 Samuel 2:21, we see how God rewards Hannah for her faith and obedience.

a. What gifts did He give her?

_____

b. Did she reject them or think of them as a burden?

_____

c. What can we learn from these examples?

_____

_____

Talk Tips

- Do you really believe that children are a blessing from God?
- Have you rejected God's potential blessings or feared being open to receiving another blessing if He wills it for you? Have you been using natural family planning selfishly, without truly being open to God's plan?
- Have you stopped enjoying your children for who they are and how they think?
- Do you appreciate your children's sense of make-believe and imagination?
- Do you spend time playing with your children? Do you explore nature with them, or go on long walks with them?

- Do you fail to enjoy your children because you are overly anxious about working to pay for unnecessary possessions and daycare?
- Have you lost sight of God's plan for you as a married couple?

Action Points

- We want to challenge you to pray and consider God's will for your fertility. Humbly ask God to shower you with the gifts of the Holy Spirit so that you will be able to discern whether you have a just and serious reason to postpone having more children. If you find that you don't, then pray for an open heart and mind to accept God's blessing, if He should bless you with another child.

Chapter 7

Raising the
Next Generation

O ne of the most chilling passages in Scripture is Judges 2:10. To experience the full impact of this passage, we need to know its context. The people of Israel, for two generations, had experienced some of the most powerful acts of God in history. First, Moses had led the people out of Egypt through the Red Sea. In addition, bread came down from heaven to feed them, and water poured miraculously from a large rock to quench their thirst. Then Joshua followed in Moses' steps. As Moses had parted the Red Sea, Joshua parted the Jordan River, and the Israelites passed through on dry land into the promised land. When the Israelites encountered the impenetrable fortress at Jericho, they conquered not by military might, but by a religious service. After several days of prayer, the priests blew their horns and the walls of Jericho, which were thick enough to race chariots on, simply exploded from the inside. No two generations saw God's active involvement in history in a more powerful way.

This is the background of Judges 2:10. Then "there arose another generation after them, who did not know the LORD" (Judges 2:10). The entire purpose of God's miraculous actions had been to lead Israel to know Him, and in just one generation all was lost! Why? A generation of parents had failed to raise up their children in godliness. Our task of giving the faith to our children is vitally important.

Listen to God as He explains why He chose Abraham to be our forefather in the faith:

[F]or I have chosen him, that he may charge his children and his household after him to keep the way of the LORD by doing righteousness and justice; so that the LORD may bring to Abraham what he has promised him (Gen. 18:19).

Parenting may be the most challenging activity we have ever attempted. So many difficult decisions—if only kids came with a handbook. But they do!

Know the Goal

All scripture is inspired by God and profitable for teaching, for reproof, for correction, and for training in righteousness, that the man of God may be complete, equipped for every good work (2 Tim. 3:16-17).

When we are told that we can be equipped for every good work, that includes raising children. But if we are going to use the Scriptures effectively, they must be read within the heart of the Church. Scripture does not provide a question-and-answer format, but rather narratives in which God fathers the great men and women of salvation history. Our heavenly Father trains His Chosen People: They succeed, they also stumble, and they are disciplined. We can learn a great deal from watching God raise His children. However, it is not as if the Bible has an index in the back of the book, so that when your ten-year-old son won't practice the piano as he has been told, you can look up "not practicing piano" and be told what to do. We need to learn the truths as they are illustrated within the narratives and clarified in precepts.

Sure, it's nice to have your children do as they are told, but we eventually want to train them so that they can make their own wise decisions. We will have failed if our thirty-year-old son or daughter is unable to function in life without Mother's direction. So, too, God is training us, in Christ, so that we actually think for ourselves, not apart from God, but because we have been formed in godliness.

No longer do I call you servants, for the servant does not know what his master is doing; but I have called you friends, for all that I have heard from my Father I have made known to you (Jn. 15:15).

Put quite simply, God has called us not to raise children, but to raise up adults who will become saints. Because of this, we must never let immediate circumstances blind us to our ultimate goal.

Our goal is not to make our children be our buddies today. Our goal is that our sons and daughters will grow up to be followers of Jesus Christ, men and women of virtue, and be with us in the presence of our heavenly Father forever. This means that we sometimes have to make unpopular decisions.

Know the Way

The $64,000 question in modern parenting is, Should you spank your children? When Archbishop Fulton J. Sheen was asked whether parents should spank their disobedient children, he responded, "They don't call it child rearing for nothing." These days, sincere parents are divided over this issue. Scripture seems to support the reasonable use of corporal punishment as a legitimate tool for parents to use (cf. Prov. 13:24; 19:18; 22:6, 15; 23:13). However, abuses of corporal punishment make it necessary to point out some guidelines.

First, don't spank out of anger. In other words, don't spank to get even. All discipline, if it is to be godly, must have the aim of restoration, not retaliation.

Second, don't spank for mistakes or minor misbehavior. The purpose of a spanking is to send a clear message that some forms of behavior are unacceptable, such as direct disobedience or blasphemy.

Third, discipline should end with restoration and healing. This is not the same thing as punishing and then retracting, which will confuse children and weaken parental authority. However, once the discipline has taken place we must always reaffirm our love for our children despite their misbehavior.

> For the moment all discipline seems painful rather than pleasant; later it yields the peaceful fruit of righteousness to those who have been trained by it (Heb. 12:11).

We have friends, whom we respect very much, who have decided never to spank their children. We respect their decision. However, some people can take this position too far. They say that it is wrong, in principle, for any parent to use corporal punishment. Michaelann and I like to think of the analogy of a golf bag. When I go out golfing, one of the clubs I bring is my sand wedge. I hope that I don't have to use this club, as that would mean that I have mishit the ball into a sand trap. While I don't want to use my sand wedge, it would be wrong for someone to tell me that I can't take it with me in my golf bag. However, if I decide to use my sand wedge, I have to use it effectively, or I could actually make matters worse. If parents decide that corporal punishment is called for in a certain circumstance, the above principles will help to ensure that their actions don't make matters worse.

The ideal of training up holy children is wonderful, but there's more. The Church gives us the tools to be successful in our efforts. She provides us the grace that comes from the sacraments and prayer and the wisdom of Scripture as understood in light of Church teaching. We have also been blessed with good mentors, exemplary Christian families that we have tried to learn from, who have helped us in this task of raising our children to be saints. All of us would like to find good families and virtuous children for ours to play with and learn from. How much more wonderful it would be if our children were the ones that others wanted around their children. This is not too much to expect or strive for, because "with God all things are possible" (Mt. 19:26).

It is difficult to find the best means for training our children because each family (as well as each child) is so different. But having wise counsel and the Word of God to use as guidelines has been very helpful. It is very important that each couple devise their own family game plan and then commit to being consistent. Steve and Karen Wood have provided some great teachings for parents. According to Steve:

> The goal of child training and discipline is to move the child from a self-centered orientation to a God-centered orientation. The only time that the rod should be used is in situations where the child willfully challenges a parent's authority, or where there is exhibition of a lack of respect for those in authority. Sporadic blowups are counterproductive in producing godly children. Your children need the secure boundaries formed by calm and consistent discipline. Sometimes you will really need to make the effort to discipline your child when you least feel like it.[1]

Keep Your Eye on the Ball

One particular strategy that we have found incredibly helpful has been the "Yes, Daddy (Mommy)" practice. Early in our parenting we found ourselves falling into the counting game: "One, two, three; now you are in trouble." Friends of ours pointed out that this can actually undermine our relationship with our kids, for we were training them not to take us seriously until we got to "three."

Our hope is that our children will respond promptly and cheerfully, and we think we have found a better way to reinforce the type of behavior we are looking for. Now we try to ask politely, and when our children hear us, they are to respond, "Yes, Dad (Mom)." This way, we know that they have heard us, and they know we expect their obedience. Their prompt response has ushered in a new era of peace in our home, and I know they can sense the difference as well.

---

[1] Steve Wood, "The Training and Discipline of Children" (talk presented at the Focus on the Catholic Family Conference, Long Beach, Calif., November 2-3, 1991).

Our kids thrive on our attention, and it can be challenging to give attention to our kids. It is not enough to be in the same room; attention means turning off the television, putting down our reading, and really keying in on them. Eye contact, real conversation, and displays of affection are all part of authentic parenting. It can be a challenge to try to engage a four year old in a conversation; he may have to repeat a single sentence several times as he searches for the right words to convey his thoughts. Nevertheless, if we can invest our time and our attention into our children, many of the disciplinary problems we fear may never arise. And if they do, they will be more easily addressed.

Stay the Course

While children have good days and bad days, we can all recognize recurring patterns of behavior in them. For the sake of discussion, it is possible to say that there are three different types of children.

The first type includes the children that nobody really enjoys having around because they behave poorly and have little respect for authority or discipline. These children often talk back to their parents, act rudely in public, and have few good manners by which they live.

The second type includes the children that others enjoy having around because they are respectful and well behaved. These are children that you don't mind bringing to an adult gathering. They are generally polite and respectful of their parents and authority figures and usually get along well with the other children.

The final type of child is the one who not only is polite and gets along well with the other children, but also actually teaches other children through his or her example how to be better—even holy. These are the children with whom parents actually look for opportunities to get their children together, because they are well on their way to becoming holy men and women.

Our children's behavior is important. Not only does it reflect our parenting, but it also reflects their awareness of God and His love and authority over all His creatures. We have had the great opportunity of experiencing all three types of children. Can you guess which ones we enjoy the most? Can you guess which type of child we should strive, with God's grace, to train up and raise? This is an awesome task and a great responsibility. We think parenting is the most difficult and challenging task that God has entrusted to us, ever! It is so great a task that He has given us the grace through the Sacrament of Marriage to succeed and form these little souls for His Kingdom: "Through the grace of the sacrament of marriage, parents receive the responsibility and privilege of *evangelizing their children*" (Catechism no. 2225, original emphasis).

Personal Application

The Book of Proverbs is full of great advice on living good and holy lives. There are specific examples given for parents on the instruction of our children that we would like to highlight in this lesson.

1. Read Proverbs 22:6. What are we as parents called to do?

_____

_____

2. Summarize Proverbs 4:1-10.

_____

_____

3. Why and when do we need to train and discipline our children?

_____

_____

4. What do Proverbs 13:24; 19:18; and 29:17 tell us?

_____

_____

5. What do 1 Corinthians 12:4-8 and Romans 12:4-8 teach us about parenting?

_____

_____

6. How are we to train and discipline our children?

_____

_____

7. Reread Proverbs 4:1; 4:10; and 29:15-17.

a. How are we told to teach?

_____

_____

b. What are children instructed to do?

_____

8. Read Deuteronomy 6:4-7. What do these verses teach us about parenting?

_____

_____

9. According to Proverbs 1:8-9, how should children treat their parents?

_____

_____

10. Read Proverbs 3:11-12 and 4:10-27 and summarize what children are instructed to do.

_____

_____

_____

11. Read Proverbs 15:31-32.

a. Whom must parents obey?

_____

_____

b. Does it really matter?

_____

_____

12. What does Matthew 18:5-6 tell us?

_____

_____

_____

13. What does Saint Paul tell us in Galatians 6:7 about our efforts?

_____

14. Take courage; we have help! Read Romans 8:28.

a. How are we supposed to accomplish all of this? Is it possible?

_____

_____

b. Whom did Christ send to help us in His absence?

_____

15. As parents, we must have the courage to lead our children. According to 1 Samuel 15:24, why did Saul fail?

_____

_____

Talk Tips

- Are your children the type of children that others enjoy having around?
- Are you serious about training up soldiers for the Kingdom of God? Are you raising your children to become saints?
- What steps do you think you need to take as parents in order to better train and form your children as God's ambassadors?

Action Points

- Schedule a time to speak with your spouse about how you're raising your children. Develop a game plan for each child to assist him (or her) in becoming a man (or woman) of faith and virtue.
- It is important to have one-on-one time with each child. We try to schedule one lunch a month with Dad, and it is equally important to have Dad watch the kids after work or on weekends so Mom can schedule one-on-one time with each child as well. These trips can be as simple as running an errand. The key is individual time.
- What do you want your family to stand for? Work on a mission statement for your family.

Chapter 8
Money Matters

Married couples seem to have a difficult time with money management:

- 49% don't pay their bills on time
- 65% don't do a good job of staying out of debt
- 65% don't balance their checkbook
- 82% don't adequately save for the future
- charitable giving averages less than 2% for all Americans and about 1% for Catholics in America. . . .
- a majority of those getting divorces point to finances as one of the primary causes of their breakup[1]

We are convinced that financial problems are not one of the primary causes of divorce, but we do think that financial problems result from many of the same problems that undermine a marriage. All of us must decide whether we will choose to live self-willed lives or Christ-centered lives. Which decision we make will affect both our family and our finances. The Scriptures give us some clear guidelines on how we can begin turning over every aspect of our lives to the lordship of Christ.

Recently, I (Curtis) was speaking to a friend of mine, and he asked me how things were going with FOCUS. I jokingly said that if he would send us a donation, we would start sending him our quarterly updates. He responded that money was tight, and he really wasn't able to give anything right now. On a more serious note, I responded that God has promised to bless us if we give,

---

[1] Philip Lenahan, *Finances for Today's Cathlic Family* (Temecula, Calif.: Financial Foundations for the Family, 1996), 7.

not the other way around. I think many Catholics may be a bit confused about this point. We often think that we could be more generous if we had more to give, but that is not what Scripture says. Jesus praises the woman who gives her last coins as having given more than those who gave greater sums out of their surplus (cf. Mk. 12:41-44). He also promises that those who are faithful in little will be given more, but those who are not, will have what little they have taken away (cf. Mt. 25:29).

There are two main steps that will help free couples who are struggling with their finances. The first may seem almost crazy, the second may seem unbelievable. Together, these two steps will liberate you to experience the freedom of Christ in this area of your life:

- If you are struggling with not having enough money, you may need to give more money away. I know that this sounds crazy, but it very well may be true. This is not a prosperity Gospel which promises financial wealth in return for faithfulness, but it is part of seeing that when we try to live a self-willed life with our finances, we may be robbing ourselves of the opportunity to be blessed by God.

- Live within your financial means, debt free.

The Tithe That Binds

We remember hearing that at the end of our life, there are two great books that will reveal who we have truly been. The first is the great book of life (cf. Rev. 20), which Our Lord will open. The second is our checkbook, which gives a penetrating insight into our values. Our personal finances are a very personal matter. Why is this? What we do with our money says a lot about who we are. As we strive to move from a self-willed life to a Christ-centered life, we find that setting things right in our finances is an important step.

The biblical step to setting our finances aright is tithing. There is a significant amount of confusion about tithing. What is a tithe?

Who is it for? How much should I give? According to Scripture, a tithe is a gift offered in support of the priests and priestly people—the Levites (cf. Num. 18:21). Not all Levites were priests. Only the men from age twenty-five to fifty-five who could prove that they had ten generations of pure Levitical blood in their veins could be priests, but the whole tribe of Levi was a priestly people. Today, an equivalent might be all priests and those who serve the Church: religious sisters and brothers, missionaries, and groups that serve the Kingdom of God. Even before the tribe of Levi was set apart as priests, Abraham offered a tenth of all that he had to the priest Melchizedek as a symbol of his covenantal faithfulness to God (cf. Gen. 14:18-20).

Biblically, a tithe serves two purposes. First, it supports the Church. But, more importantly, a tithe is a symbolic gesture of recognition that all that we have really belongs to God. By offering the first tenth back to God through the Church, we manifest our faith in God that we trust in Him, and not in what He has allowed us to acquire. God's true desire is to be generous with us, but even more, as a loving Father, He wants us to imitate Him in generous love.

Scripture does more than teach what a tithe is. The Bible shows how central this simple act of faith is to a healthy spiritual life. The prophet Malachi calls the people of Israel to repent and return to God. In his prophecy, he outlines a number of areas in which the people have been unfaithful. In fact, the Book of Malachi is wonderful reading for families today, for it deals with topics like religious loyalty, marital faithfulness, divorce, father-son relationships, and other timely topics. In the prophecy, God answers the people's question about why He has been so far away from them:

> From the days of your fathers you have turned aside from my statutes and have not kept them. Return to me, and I will return to you, says the LORD of hosts. But you say, "How shall we return?" Will man rob God? Yet you are robbing me. But you say,

"How are we robbing thee?" In your tithes and offerings. You are cursed with a curse, for you are robbing me; the whole nation of you. Bring the full tithes into the storehouse, that there may be food in my house; and thereby put me to the test, says the LORD of hosts, if I will not open the windows of heaven for you and pour down for you an overflowing blessing (Mal. 3:7-10).

The language of God is very strong: Those who are not tithing are referred to as robbing God. Upon closer examination, we find an amazing promise in this passage. Ordinarily, it is a sin to "put God to the test" (cf. Deut. 6:16; Mt. 4:7). Here, we read the one exception to this definition of sin: We are told that we should test God in this matter. If we bring our whole tithe, He will provide us with an overflowing blessing. One might object, "This is the Old Testament; it is outdated." Note the verse immediately before the passage we just read: "For I the LORD do not change; therefore you, O sons of Jacob, are not consumed" (Mal. 3:6). Scripture is clear that our God is unchanging, and He is calling us to trust Him with our entire lives, including our finances.

The beautiful thing is that His challenge comes with a promise. In our marriage, we have tried to take God at His Word on this point and He has proven Himself faithful. Several years ago, before we were married, when I (Curtis) was an undergraduate in school, I had very little income. It was near the end of my senior year, and I was looking through a Catholic magazine. I knew that I had less than $100 left in my account, but as I read on, I felt compelled to give some money to a group of missionary priests. I went to get my checkbook, but when I returned to the magazine, I looked and looked, but I could not find the advertisement for the priests anywhere. Finally, I decided that I would go ahead and write a $25 check to an order of nuns. After I wrote the check, I tossed the magazine on my bed. The magazine fell open to the page with the priests. It seemed apparent to me that this was a little test; I decided this was an opportunity to trust God, even if I wasn't sure how He would provide. I wrote a second check for $25 and put each into an envelope. I walked out to the mailbox and discovered that I had a letter from my mom waiting for me. I had just given $50 away and to my great surprise, my mother had unexpectedly sent me $500. Even more amazingly, although I had just given $50, I had actually written two $25 checks and inside my mother's letter was not one check for $500, but two checks for $250 each.

Later, after Michaelann and I were married, we went away to graduate school. We thought God had called me to study theology, but leaving work in California to become an unemployed, young married student family wasn't easy. By this time we had two children. After much prayer, we decided to go, with the understanding that graduate school was a luxury and that I would do what I could to provide. If we missed a single meal, then I would drop out of school and go back to work full time. During school, we remained committed to tithing. It was sometimes difficult to give 10 percent of our income, when some months our income may have been only $500. One time, we were so broke that we had to turn down a dinner invitation because we couldn't afford the gas to drive to our friends' house.

Finally, the day arrived. We were broke and out of food. Up until this time, we had never missed a meal. We knew that the next morning I would have to withdraw from school. There was nothing left to do, and then we heard a knock on the door. When we opened the door, a friend was standing there with a large pot. She said, "I made way too much spaghetti tonight, could you all use some?" We had spaghetti that night and again for lunch the next day. That afternoon, an unexpected reimbursement check came in the mail. God had provided.

Another frequently asked question is, Can I give 2 percent or 5 percent? Of course you can, but if you give 5 percent that is not a tithe; it is a "fifthe." A tithe literally comes from a tenth, or 10 percent. A tithe is offering back the first 10 percent of your income to God.

The Church does not require Catholics to tithe. The Catechism teaches that the fifth precept of the Church is that "the faithful are obliged to assist with the material needs of the Church, each according to his own ability" (Catechism, no. 2043). However, God has blessed our attempts to tithe, and we invite you to take up His challenge and see if He will not open up the windows of heaven for you as well. The beauty of tithing is that it is one area where we know if we are on track or not. It is one thing to say, "From now on, I won't lose my temper," and another thing to restrain our anger consistently. However, once we made the decision to tithe, it has been easy to see whether we are still on track. The numbers don't lie.

Living Free of Debt

Earlier, we had mentioned that there were two steps to beginning to experience the freedom of Christ in your financial lives. We warned that the idea of tithing might, at first, appear crazy. The next step, living within our financial means, might at first seem impossible. Living free of debt, however, not only is possible, but also may allow you the freedom to earn over a quarter of a million dollars—an odd claim for a Scripture study! Before we examine this next step, we need to take a brief look at freedom.

As Americans we tend to confuse freedom with independence. After all, did not America gain its freedom with a Declaration of Independence? But the freedom Christ offers is very different from what we might first think. We have just seen that the Bible promises that God will bless us if we offer our tithe as an act of faith. The blessing God promises will actually increase our freedom, but not our independence. We need to rethink freedom from the Christian perspective.

Several years ago, I (Curtis) injured my ear playing basketball. As the doctor was sewing up my cut, I asked him, "Doc, will I be able to play the violin?" He assured me that I would, and I told him that this was a miracle, because I had never been able to play it before.

You see, I am not free to play the violin. I have not trained; I have neither the know-how nor the necessary skills. Only someone who has committed himself to training and practicing the violin has the freedom to play. So, too, with authentic freedom: Only those who have committed themselves to a Christ-centered life and are living the life of grace can experience what Jesus called freedom.

During the Middle Ages, some feudal lords, in a manner of speaking, enslaved working serfs. After months of work in the field, the lords would simply collect their share. Modern Americans are proud to be free. However, many of us have unwittingly chosen to become modern-day serfs. Many families expend over two-thirds of their income between taxes and servicing their personal debt. Couples enticed by the promise of easy credit find themselves enslaved by monthly payments. Between consumer debt (credit cards), car loans, and home loans, many families have scarcely anything left. There must be a better way. Couples, particularly young couples, need to avoid the easy-credit trap.

This may seem like an unusual topic for a Bible study, but the Scriptures actually warn against charging usury on a loan (that is, money earned on a loan up and beyond compensation for inflation and risk). The Judeo-Christian condemnation against usury was consistent from the time of Moses until the Protestant Reformation. At that time, John Calvin broke with thousands of years of tradition and the clear teaching of Sacred Scripture and accepted usury. But the concept of usury is still based upon a lie, and if spouses aren't careful, they will become ensnared in its trap.

Let's look at three major areas in which most people don't think twice about spending money they haven't yet earned: credit card spending, home loans, and car loans.

Credit Cards

The average American family has $8,523 in credit card debt. If they paid only their minimum payment, and charged nothing else, it would take years to pay off their debt, and they would have to pay an additional $5,184 in interest. And new purchases would be subject to immediate and exorbitant interest charges.[2]

Home Loans

Imagine a young couple deciding to purchase a house for $180,000. They put $20,000 down on the home and borrow the remaining $160,000 at 7 percent interest over thirty years. In the end, they will have paid $403,214.24 for their $180,000 house. That means that if the couple is at a 25 percent tax rate, they will actually need to earn more than $475,000 to buy their $180,000 home! They still might choose to buy the house, but they should realize the true cost.

Here is another concept that many couples fail to consider. If their monthly payment is $1,064.40, how much will it cost them to double their payment? It will actually cost them only about $150! Here's how: The principal actually paid down with the first payment is only $131.15. By adding $131.92 to their payment (the amount of principal that would have been paid on the second payment), they could actually eliminate an entire additional payment of over $1,060. If the couple increased their payment to $1,438.13 per month (only $373.73 a month more), they could pay off their house fifteen years earlier and save $124,351.70! If they buy a more modest home and make more aggressive payments, they can increase the savings even more.

---

[2] Mellody Hobson, "Make It Count: Invest This Year's Dollars with Care," abc NEWS.com (January 2, 2002), http://abcnews.go.com/sections/GMA/GoodMorning America/GMA020102FinancialResolutions.html.

Car Loans

Cars, in a sense, are even more expensive. The interest rate is typically higher, the interest is not deductible, and the car is depreciating in value. A $200,000 home may be worth $220,000 after five years, showing a $20,000 profit, whereas a $20,000 car may be worth $10,000 in five years, showing a $10,000 loss. New cars depreciate more quickly than used cars do.

For example, a $20,000 new car with a 20 percent down payment at 8 percent interest over five years actually costs $23,898.51. By the time it is paid for, the car is worth only about $10,000. Payments would have been approximately $364.98 per month, and this is before gasoline, insurance, and maintenance (possibly an additional $200 or more per month). If, instead, the couple deposited the initial down payment of $2,000 into a fund yielding 5 percent and then deposited $350 per month into the fund, the couple could have saved approximately $26,048.33 in the same five years (over $20,000 in just four years).

As you may suspect, following these principles is more difficult than just knowing them. However, as we begin to make good decisions, keeping on track actually becomes easier. Once we know how freeing it is to live as God has designed—keeping our material things in check with the priority of always giving God our first fruits, and living within our financial means—then it is easier to develop a financial plan or budget and live by it.

There have been many times that I (Michaelann) have wanted to purchase miscellaneous items impulsively, but I didn't because Curtis and I had discussed our debt-reduction plan in detail. We had given each other our word that we would commit to attaining our goal by not spending on extra items without discussing it first. At the end of this book, we have recommended some helpful books to explain the details of getting finances in order.

Personal Application

1. Read Matthew 23:23. Does Jesus criticize His audience for tithing? Is He condemning tithing in general?

_____

_____

_____

2. Read Numbers 18:21. Explain what a tithe is. Who were the priests and priestly people?

_____

_____

3. In Genesis 14:18-20, to whom does Abraham give one tenth? Why?

_____

_____

4. Read Hebrews 7:4. Whose gift is referred to as a tithe?

_____

5. What does Sirach 35:9 tell us?

_____

6. Read Malachi 3:7-10.

a. What do these verses teach us?

_____

b. How does God view the failure to tithe?

_____

c. What does God instruct His People to do?

_____

_____

7. At times, we as Christians think that talk of money is not spiritual, but Our Lord has some challenging things to say about money management. Let's look at Luke 18:24 and 1 Timothy 6:10.

a. Even though these statements are harsh, what is their true meaning?

_____

_____

b. Upon a more careful look, do you think money is the problem, or is it a disordered use or love of money that is?

_____

_____

8. Scripture teaches about credit in Proverbs 22:7. What does it say about the one who borrows?

_____

_____

9. Let's examine the Scriptures to see what they teach about usury. Read Exodus 22:25; Leviticus 25:36; Nehemiah 5:7; Psalm 15:5; and Ezekiel 18:4-9, 13, 17. What is the common thread these verses share?

_____

_____

Talk Tips

- Have you already set financial goals, both short term and long term? If so, how realistic are they? How long has it been since you've reviewed them?
- What are your spending habits? Have you ever tracked your spending for a period of time to see in black and white where all of your money *really* goes?

- Do you currently tithe 10 percent consistently? If so, have you noticed that finances somehow seem to "work out" for you each month?

Action Points

- Discuss your financial goals.
- Then evaluate your current spending habits and monthly expenses. Philip Lenahan's easy booklet and worksheets (see the additional reading section) are helpful in developing a budget. Keep in mind that it may take a month just to get some numbers to work with.
- After you become familiar with your expenses, decide on your tithe together, and then set goals. We set short-term goals: paying off our credit cards and not using them anymore, then paying off our car. We set long-term goals as well: paying off our hefty student loans, working on the mortgage payment, and saving for retirement and college. It is so important to put this plan of attack into a short-term and long-term perspective. It has helped us to talk about the budget every few months, too. We have celebrated when each goal has been met, and talking about our plans keeps us focused and motivated to keep plugging away when debt reduction seems so monotonous. It also reunites us in our common goal and strengthens our marriage in knowing that we are each sacrificing to attain our goals. This is a tall order, but the rewards for investing the time and energy are great!

Chapter 9
Restoring
Catholic Culture

Raising kids can be dirty work. At least that's the way we like to think of it. We have gained great insight from Our Lord's parable of the sower (cf. Lk. 8:4-15). In the parable, Jesus compares four different types of soils: the pathway, the rocky ground, the thorns, and the good soil. God scatters His seed on each type of soil, but only the seed that falls into the good soil ends up bearing abundant fruit. As parents, we are all called to prepare the soil of our children's hearts, so that they may receive God's Word and bear abundant fruit. We must also make the effort to break up the rocky soil and clear out the weeds of this world: materialism, inappropriate television shows, unmonitored Internet access, bad peer groups, and so forth. We are called to cultivate virtue and root out vice, so that our children's souls will become fertile soil. This is a daunting task, and we can't possibly succeed without the help of God and His grace.

The role of parents in education is of such importance that it is almost impossible to provide an adequate substitute. The right and duty of parents to educate their children is primordial and inalienable. Parents are the principal and first educators of their children (Catechism, nos. 1653, 2221).

We were both raised in Catholic homes. We went to Mass on Sundays and holy days, and we received religious education through our parishes and at home. Michaelann even attended Catholic school, but in our teens, we both struggled with our faith. It is all too common to find young Catholics drifting away from the Church. What they need is to have the soil of their hearts cultivated.

We are so convinced of this that we spend most of our time working with FOCUS. Our main goal is to share the reasons for hope that the Catholic Church provides (cf. 1 Pet. 3:15). FOCUS equips young missionaries with the tools to lead Bible studies, to answer questions, and to lead others to the fullness of our faith. It is very challenging work, but God continues to provide for our needs while allowing us to see the fruit of our efforts as well. If our work with college students proves anything to us, it is that young people hunger for the life-changing truth of Jesus Christ.

We have seen how the truth of Sacred Scripture can transform lives. One key component of our work with young people is to show them how the sacred liturgy brings us into the life of Christ, that the Mass is the Gospel made present in time. The liturgical year is designed as a tool to live, love, and understand more fully the abundant life Christ has given us.

Precisely because we are called to a personal relationship with Jesus, we are called to be in the world but not of the world. It isn't only college students who need a Christ-centered worldview. When we had our first son, Brock, we began to see how important it was for us to pass on our faith by cultivating a Christ-centered worldview within him from his earliest years.

Michaelann began to discover that the liturgical year provided a great tool to allow us to live the life of Christ every day throughout the year. Unfortunately, information about family customs based upon the liturgical year isn't easy to find. After spending years gathering ideas about to how to live the Christian faith within our home, Michaelann coauthored *The Catholic Parent Book of Feasts* with Carol Puccio and Zoë Romanowsky. The book describes timeless customs and adapts them to our modern world. We need to find whatever sources we can to restore a Catholic sense to our life and to our world.

The Power of Prayer

The *Christian family* is the first place for education in prayer. . . .
For young children in particular, daily family prayer is the first
witness of the Church's living memory as awakened patiently by
the Holy Spirit (Catechism, no. 2685, original emphasis).

C. S. Lewis once referred to Christianity as a "good infection."[1]
Our goal in parenting is to become contagious. In other words,
our primary objective in life is to go to heaven and take as many
people with us as we can. There are two helpful disciplines in
becoming a contagious Christian: study and prayer. Study
transforms our thoughts, and prayer transforms our hearts. When
we pray and develop a deeper relationship with Our Lord, He
begins to work through us by "infecting" others with our living
faith. More than anything, we want to be sure that our children
catch a good case of Christianity.

The great saints have always understood the transforming
power of prayer. Saint Peter of Alcantara speaks beautifully of how
the soul is perfected by drawing close to God through prayer:

In mental prayer the soul is purified from its sins, nourished with
charity, confirmed in faith, and strengthened in hope; the mind
expands, the affections dilate, the heart is purified, truth becomes
evident; temptation is conquered, sadness dispelled; the senses are
renovated; drooping powers revive; tepidity ceases; the rust of
vices disappears. Out of mental prayer issues [*sic*] forth, like living sparks, those desires of heaven which the soul conceives when
inflamed with the fire of divine love. Sublime is the excellence of
mental prayer, great are its privileges; to mental prayer heaven is
opened; to mental prayer heavenly secrets are manifested and the
ear of God ever attentive.[2]

---

[1] *Mere Christianity* (San Francisco: Harper, 2001), 172.
[2] Saint Peter of Alcantara, *Treatise on Prayer*, part 1, in Rev. Peter-Thomas Rohrbach,
O.C.D., *Conversation with Christ: An Introduction to Mental Prayer* (Chicago: Fides
Publishers, 1956), 13.

Sacramental Grace: Our Secret Weapon

Remember for a moment when you fell in love with your spouse. Wasn't it wonderful anticipating spending time together? I (Michaelann) remember bathing extra long, choosing just the right outfits, making sure that I was presenting myself in the best possible way. Curtis would even go so far as to wash and clean his car before each date. We can have that same desire to present our best selves to God as well. We have been given the wonderful Sacrament of Confession, in which Christ forgives our sins, cleanses our souls, and gives us the grace to be stronger in the face of temptation, making us more presentable before God. How often do we take advantage of the rich blessings we are offered?

Christ also continues to bestow Himself on us in the Eucharist. He desires to transform each one of us. God pours His very life into us; we receive His Son's body, blood, soul, and divinity. "The sacraments are efficacious signs of grace, instituted by Christ and entrusted to the Church, by which divine life is dispensed to us" (Catechism, no. 1131).

The Family That Prays
(and Fasts) Together Stays Together

We have been working for years to develop "the Martin way." It is up to spouses to find out what will be their family's way. While each family is different, there are certain elements we have found very effective. In our family, we like to stress the liturgical year and the lives of the saints. We try to incorporate the liturgical year by remembering the feast day of each of the children's patron saints. Baptismal days are a bigger deal than birthdays. We change our tablecloth colors as they coincide with the colors of the liturgical calendar (for example, violet during Lent), and the children notice the same colors as we attend Mass.

As our children grow older, we are trying to establish a family reading time. We have tried to include the classics as well as many of the lives of the saints. Our goal is to have the children venture off on their own to do more individual reading about these great heroes and heroines of our faith.

In addition, we try to foster the growth of virtue in our children. Every week or so, we focus on a new virtue. Just recently, we had been working, for about five days, on the virtue of respect. Michaelann had just asked our son Augustine to do a chore. He began to whine, and then caught himself, and said, "I'm sorry, Mom; that wasn't very respectful." It is always a joy to see some progress in your work of cultivating the soil of a heart.

Personal Application

1. Read Romans 12:1-2.

a. What choice must we make? How ought we to be transformed?

_____

_____

_____

b. What tools do we have to obey these instructions?

_____

_____

2. Jesus gives us the example of His prayer life. Read Matthew 26:36-45; Mark 1:35; 6:46-47; Luke 5:16; 6:12; and John 17.

a. When, where, and how did Jesus pray?

_____

_____

b. How can we use His example and imitate it in our own lives?

_____

_____

3. In Matthew 25:31-46, Christ tells us what to expect at the final judgment. What type of customs or activities can we implement in our families to live as Christ expects His followers to live?

_____

_____

4. Read Hebrews 13:2. How does this verse encourage us to serve those in need?

_____

_____

Talk Tips

- At Sunday dinner, ask each of your children to mention a way he could become more like Christ. Then ask for ideas about what the family could do. Take some of these ideas, and make them your action points.
- Discuss and decide upon the best time for your family prayer.
- As a couple, talk about ways that you might better pass on the faith to your children. Could you incorporate the liturgical year more effectively? Could you begin to read about the saints together or get a child's picture Bible and begin to read and learn Bible stories as a family?

Action Points

- Arrange to have a family meeting where everyone comes together to discuss how your family can better serve God. You could visit an elderly neighbor or make cookies to cheer up someone. The older kids could offer free baby-sitting for a new mom, or mow the lawn for an elderly neighbor . . . the ideas are nearly infinite! Just think of ways to be like Christ, to serve, and to give of self.

- Recommit yourself to a time for personal prayer. Then talk to your spouse about how you can encourage each other in prayer. Recommit your family to a prayer time together.
- Take out a calendar and mark family feasts, name days (the feast days of patron saints), and so forth, to begin to celebrate the Church's liturgical year in your home.

Chapter 10
We're on a Mission from God

If we take a moment to return to C. S. Lewis's analogy of the three ships, we can plot our personal course to heaven. We've examined how to become seaworthy vessels. We've tried to set forth effective tactics so as not to crash into one another, but rather honor one another and work side by side to build a successful marriage and family. We want to complete our study by recognizing that God has specific plans for our family. It is so important that each of us realize that we are all on a mission from God.

We have had the great opportunity to receive input from families across the country as we prepared this study. Some have been engaged couples; others have been married for more than thirty years. All have offered valuable advice, and all have in common the married vocation and mission to get themselves, their spouses, their families, and as many others as possible to heaven. This is what it all comes down to. Are we willing to take the challenge? It doesn't have to be a daunting task—it can be seen as a great adventure!

The challenge will be in how we take the fruit of this study and apply it to our marriage and family life. The first step is to embrace our faith with a spirit of joy. Knowing that we are God's children, that He wants to bless us in this life, and that He wants us to be with Him for all of eternity should affect every aspect of our life. We have found that the most contagious Catholics are those who are joyful. They do simple things like smile and have a way of being positive even in the most difficult situations. This doesn't just happen; it takes effort. As someone once said, "Sow a thought, reap an action; sow an action, and reap a habit; sow a habit and reap a character; sow a character and reap a destiny."

The people who make the effort to have good and holy thoughts will manifest their thoughts in good and holy actions. Their actions will become habits, so that no matter where they are or what they are doing, their lives will be permeated by their faith. Often, when we see great character in other people, we want to be more like them. It all makes perfect sense, too: God made us to rejoice in the good and holy, and it is natural to appreciate goodness and holiness in others. It is hard work to do it ourselves, but we can take courage knowing that others will see the good in us, and they, too, might want this joy and happiness for themselves, thus making our faith contagious. It is all a part of this great mission that we are on.

The Right to Be Heard

By struggling to live our faith well, we earn the right to be heard. Pope John Paul II has been able to speak to a divided world about life, justice, truth, and Jesus Christ. Not everyone has accepted his preaching, but when someone who lives the truth speaks, his life is a witness to his speech. So, too, with Mother Teresa. She was probably one of the most respected women to have lived in our lifetime, and everyone saw value in her life. By living her life in such a selfless way, she earned respect, honor, and the right to be heard. When she pointed to President Bill Clinton and told him abortion was wrong, everyone listened. He may not have changed his position, but he had no right or place to argue or respond because she had earned the right to speak the truth. Mother Teresa wasn't known for spouting her opinions to the world. She was a woman of action and very few words. But when asked, she knew what to say and how to say it. This confidence comes only from prayer and a deep relationship with God.

Like Pope John Paul II and Mother Teresa, we too can bear effective witness to the faith. People will watch us and question us because they want to know what we are doing, not only because it is attractive but also because it is honorable and good. It is difficult to live as Christ-centered families in a society that all too often contradicts truth, beauty, goodness, and all that is holy. But it is not impossible: "I can do all things in him who strengthens me" (Phil. 4:13).

Being humble is an integral part of the right to be heard. We have all been around those people that feel the need to spout their opinions about everything all the time. They are the ones you try to avoid sitting next to at potluck dinners because they talk your ear off. Usually, those are not the people that others are going to want to imitate. The easiest people to learn from are those who live their faith but do not boast about it. They realize that they owe everything to God and His grace.

Put Out into the Deep

We are all called to evangelize. In doing so, we need to avoid two extremes: being arrogant or boastful, and being silent when we ought to speak up. Pope John Paul II has reminded the faithful of the call to evangelize time and time again during his pontificate, and he has also stressed that we need to have the heart of Christ as we do so.

At the beginning of our study, we considered the analogy of the ships. Each of us is like a ship sailing towards the same destination. Each family is like a small fleet of ships. Society is like a very large battalion of ships. We hope to be seaworthy and not crash into others, but unfortunately many ship captains out there don't know the final destination. It is up to us to share with them the Good News that God has entrusted to us.

Where can they go to hear the Good News? How can they arrive at their destination most effectively? These questions become of great concern to us when we realize that evangelization is part of our mission as a family. We can help spread the Gospel by hosting Bible studies in our homes or by becoming more involved in our parishes. Finding friends who share the same insights and goals is also very helpful, since many hands make light work.

Personal Application

1. What does 1 Peter 3:8-17 tell us about evangelization?

_____

_____

2. Read the invitation of Pope John Paul II to become a coworker with Christ:

> [I]t is especially necessary to recognize the unique place that, in this field, belongs to the mission of married couples and Christian families, by virtue of the grace received in the sacrament. This mission must be placed at the service of the building up of the Church, the establishing of the Kingdom of God in history. . . . This apostolate will be exercised in the first place within . . . families. . . . The apostolate of the family will also become wider through works of spiritual and material charity towards other families.[1]

What decisions can we make to help other families come to discover the blueprint for lasting joy in the family?

_____

_____

3. According to Genesis 18:19, why was Abraham chosen to receive God's blessing?

_____

_____

---

[1] Apostolic Exhortation on the Role of the Christian Family in the Modern World _Familiaris Consortio_ (November 22, 1981), no. 71.

4. How can our families help fulfill the great commission found in Matthew 28:18-20?

_____

_____

5. In Acts 1:8, the apostles are given a game plan for implementing the great commission. They are told to begin in Judea, then go to Samaria, and then go to the "end of the earth." How can our families design a specific plan to share the Good News of Christ, beginning at home (Judea), then with your neighbors (Samaria), and finally even to the end of the earth?

_____

_____

6. According to 1 Thessalonians 2:8, what two things did Saint Paul share with the people in his life?

_____

7. Consider the example of the friendship between Saints Paul and Timothy (2 Tim. 1:3-14; 2:1-7). How important is it not only to share the teachings of Christ, but also to encourage others to do the same?

_____

_____

8. Read Titus 2:1-8. Why is it so important to live family life in an authentically Christian manner, for the sake of both our friends and non-Christians?

_____

_____

_____

_____

Talk Tips

- In your personal talk time, discuss with each other what you enjoyed the most about this study.
- Share something that you learned about your spouse that you did not know about him or her before doing this study together.
- Find some time to talk with your spouse about your mission. It might be helpful to write out your individual mission statements and then write out a family mission statement together. This is a great activity for families with older children, too. Everyone loves to be asked for his opinion and input.
- Discus whether your family is a good witness to the Catholic faith.

Action Points

- After discussing a family mission statement, take time to write it out on a poster board. Have each family member sign and date it, and hang it in a prominent place. Some families we know even frame their mission statement and hang it in the entrance of their home.
- Make an effort to evangelize others by witnessing to them and inviting them into your home. We have found that when we invite others over for dinner or board games, it is much easier to talk about our faith because they naturally are attracted to the fun and find it easy to ask questions.

Leader's Guide

As Bible study leaders ourselves, we believe that it is very beneficial to read and study additional materials to facilitate group discussion. Please see the additional reading section at the end of this book for a useful reading list.

Chapter 1

1. a. God wants to bless us and promises to bless us.
   b. God became man so that we may have life abundantly.

2. a. We go our own way and are scattered.
   b. We end up doing what we hate because we are broken.

3. a. Jesus tells us, "I am the way, and the truth, and the life."
   b. This verse tells us that "God so loved the world that he gave his only Son, that whoever believes in Him should not perish but have eternal life."

4. a. The wise man obeys and builds his house on rock; the foolish man does not obey and builds his house on sand.
   b. Jesus expects us to hear His commands and teachings and then to obey Him. We need to lay a solid foundation, beginning with our faith.
   c. Saint Peter instructs us to repent—to change fully and live our lives for Christ—and be baptized.

5. a. We are told that we shall be cleansed and be given a new heart and new spirit in Christ.
   b. 1. The apostles' teaching
      2. Fellowship
      3. The breaking of bread
      4. The prayers

Chapter 2

1. Christ gives an example of living a life with quiet times for prayer, in the morning and at night.

2. We need to make time to be alone with God and pray, speak with Him, and listen to Him.

3. a. "[S]eek first his kingdom and his righteousness."
   b. "Do not be conformed to this world, but be transformed by the renewal of your mind"—think about what is good, acceptable, and perfect.
   c. Rejoice and have no anxiety; by prayers and supplication speak with God; and let your requests be made known to Him with thanksgiving. In all things, trust that God will work for the good of those who love Him.

4. Tobit and Sarah pray together on their wedding night.

5. a. The image is of three strands not easily broken apart.
   b. (Personal reflection)
   c. 1. God
      2. The husband
      3. The wife

6. a. Where two or three are gathered in His name, there is Christ in their midst.
   b. Mary, the apostles, the women, and the brethren are praying together in the upper room.
   c. (Personal reflection)

Chapter 3

1. God is asking husbands to be faithful to their wives and honor them. Husbands need to be charitable in their words and deeds.

2. a. The wife is challenged to keep herself beautiful, inside and out, for her husband.

    b. The husband is challenged to be infatuated with his wife's love always.

3 a. We can try to renew our love for one another by being kind, thoughtful, and well groomed, and by strengthening our friendship always.

    b. One might offer to do little tasks for the other out of love and with a spirit of service. Examples might include helping with the dishes or bathing the children. (Personal reflection)

4. No, friends are called to love at all times. Jesus even goes so far as to tell us to love everyone!

5. Quarreling is likened to the bars of a castle (the dungeon)—to being in jail, trapped.

6. It is very important to talk things out and work toward resolution. We are instructed to work things out as soon as we realize there is a conflict—here and now, before the sun goes down. Resolve the conflict before the Devil destroys the relationship!

7. We need to communicate with each other with well-chosen words.

8. a. A good wife is very precious. She is trustworthy and does others good, not harm.

    b. She speaks with wisdom and kindness. She chooses her words carefully.

9. He is a man of deep purpose and understanding.

10. We are called to speak to each other in love and truth and build up each other in love. In doing so, we shall walk wisely and make the most of our time on earth and our time together.

Chapter 4

1. Satan tempted Eve with knowledge, freedom, and becoming like God. He was encouraging her to doubt in God's fatherly care.

2. a. Satan, through our modern culture, tempts us with money, power, sexual exploits, excessive pleasures, and passions.
   b. (Personal reflection)
   c. (Personal reflection)
   d. Women can embrace their femininity and vocation as wife and mother by being the heart of their home. Men can embrace their vocation as husbands and fathers by providing for their families and being the spiritual and physical heads of their homes. These vocations are challenging but God given.

3. a. Christ died for His Bride, the Church.
   b. Husbands need to be willing to lay down their lives for their wives in service to them.
   c. Wives are called to submit to their husbands as the Church submits to Christ. Each is called to submit to Christ's leadership in the home.

4. a. Jesus came to serve, to be the ransom for many souls to get to heaven.
   b. We are called to imitate His service by serving our spouse, family, and Church.

5. Jesus is teaching us to serve and be humble before God. We need to act like Christ, serve others, and teach them by our example.

6. We need to remember to serve with gladness and singing. We are called to keep a joyful heart and attitude as we serve. Acquiring the habit of smiling is a great place to start!

Chapter 5

1. **a.** Adam and Eve were made for each other and were not ashamed of their nakedness.

   b. God commanded Adam and Eve to be fruitful and multiply, to fill the earth and subdue it.

2. **a.** The wife is seen as a stream or well that belongs to her husband.

   b. This image shows us that men shouldn't wander to other women (dip into other wells) but enjoy his one well.

3. **a.** The wife is seen as a precious jewel, a locked garden, a sealed fountain that is only opened for the one and only lover.

   b. The husband's garden and fountain is his one wife.

   c. It is the wife's obligation to unlock her garden and open her fountain for her one and only love. She is his and his alone.

4. A husband is instructed to enjoy life with the wife he loves, all the days of his life.

5. It could be summed up as being present to your wife, respecting and honoring her, and enjoying being with her.

6. We need to ensure an undefiled bed. We need to remain faithful to our spouse until death.

7. Women are instructed to teach younger women wisdom, modesty, and graciousness. They are also to give instruction about marriage, and about being a good wife and mother. Part of being a good wife is awakening love at the proper time by being romantic and welcoming especially in the sacredness of the bedroom.

8. **a.** (Personal reflection to be shared with spouse)

   b. (Personal reflection to be shared with spouse)

Chapter 6

1. a. Children are like the arrows in a warrior's quiver.
   b. We are the Church militant; therefore, we are warriors for God. We need to have children and be open to their blessing upon our families in order to win the war against the culture of death and against our own sins, vices, and imperfections.

2. a. Fear of the Lord is a healthful fear of God's almighty power. It involves honoring God with a healthful and rightly-ordered love and reverence.
   b. To walk in God's ways means following His instructions.
   c. We are told in Genesis to be fruitful and multiply and subdue the earth. We need to follow these commandments and be open to life.
   d. Yes, children are a blessing, just as the olive plant is a sign of blessing in Jewish tradition.
   e. (Personal reflection)

3. a. These are stories about couples who are sorrowful because they are unable to conceive children.
   b. Their suffering is great.

4. a. God was the one in control of giving Ruth her son, Obed.
   b. King David was later born as Obed's grandson.

5. a. God was in control of her fertility.
   b. She acknowledged God's power through her heartfelt prayers.
   c. She showed her faith and humility by her prayer and supplication.
   d. She was rewarded in God's own time by having a baby.
   e. She promises to "give him to the LORD all the days of his life" and presented Samuel to God as an offering for His service.

6. **a.** God further rewarded her service and devotion with more children.

   b. No, she welcomed the children.

   c. We need to learn to trust God by being open to receiving more children as blessings.

Chapter 7

1. We are called to train up a child in the way he should go.

2. A father's instructions need to be wise and heard by the children.

3. We parents need to train our children because we want them to have life and wisdom.

4. We need to discipline our children while they are young and docile to teaching, while there is hope they can receive the teaching. (After children are trained to obey, around the time they reach the age of reason, we can use explanation and dialogue to teach them.)

5. We need to remember that God has given each of our children different gifts.

6. Fathers' instructions should be heard and understood. Then, in extreme cases of disobedience, couples need to be willing to use the rod of discipline.

7. **a.** We are told to teach by first getting our children's attention, being loving and showing sincere concern for each one. Then we are told to discipline the child with love, when needed.

   b. Children are instructed to hear the words of their father and reject not their mother's instructions.

8. We are told that parents need to teach their children to love God with their whole heart, soul, and strength. We need to do this at all times in our homes. Whether we walk, sit, or lie down (cf. Deut. 6:7), we should always teach by word and example.

9. We need to teach our children to listen and obey their parents, thus making the Fourth Commandment ("Honor your father and your mother") practical to them. Then we need to teach them that obedience is like a pendant around their neck, a jewel that pleases God, the angels, and the saints.

10. The Lord reproves him whom He loves; therefore, it is fitting that parents reprove the children whom they love. Also, children need to accept wise counsel and act upon it, for the correct path is like a light.

11. a. As parents, we are called to obey the Church, the pope, and our bishops and priests. Our obedience to them is a great example to our children, too.
    b. Yes, it always matters, for to ignore instruction is to despise ourselves.

12. When we receive children, we receive Christ. If we cause one of them to sin, it would be better for us to be drowned than to face God.

13. Whatever one sows, one also reaps.

14. a. In everything we do, God is working for the good of those who love and are called according to His purpose. So it is possible!
    b. We have the Holy Spirit to help us. What an awesome gift from God!

15. Saul failed because he preferred the ways of the people to God's law.

Chapter 8

1. Jesus criticizes His audience, not because they tithe all the right spices, but because they have neglected the weightier, more important matters like justice, mercy, and faith. Jesus wants us to tithe with a charitable heart of generosity.

2. A tithe was 10 percent of all one's goods. The tithe was given to the Levite tribe, the priestly tribe that took care of the spiritual needs of the people.

3. Abraham tithes to Melchizedek, the king of Salem, because he was the priest of God Almighty.

4. Abraham's gift to Melchizedek is described as a tithe.

5. With every gift, we need to show a cheerful face. We need to dedicate the tithe with gladness.

6. **a.** These verses teach us that God wants His people to tithe to His Church—to support her works and mission financially.
   b. God views the failure to tithe as if it were robbery.
   c. He tells us to return to Him and to offer the full tithe, to test Him in this, and He will open up heaven and pour forth blessings upon us.

7. **a.** Both readings teach us about the danger of the disordered love of money.
   b. Money itself is not the problem; there are wealthy people who are detached from their wealth and very generous. Rather, love of money and things is the problem. Love of money leads to a lack of generosity and ultimately excludes God from the material aspects of life.

8. The borrower is a slave to the lender.

9. The common thread in these passages is that exacting or charging interest on money loaned is forbidden by God (cf. Catechism, nos. 2269, 2449).

Chapter 9

1. **a.** We must choose to present our bodies as a living sacrifice, holy and acceptable for spiritual worship. Then we are told not to be conformed to this world, but be transformed by the renewal of our minds. We are transformed by His grace, which we receive through prayer and the sacraments. Our minds are renewed by the regular reading of Sacred Scripture, the Catechism, and other solid spiritual reading like the lives of the saints and the writings of the Fathers and Doctors of the Church.
   b. We have been given great tools in prayer, frequenting the sacraments, reading the Scriptures and other spiritual reading to enlighten our minds and hearts.

2. **a.** Jesus took time out of His busy schedule to be alone to pray early in the morning and in the evening. Often, He was alone; sometimes, He prayed in the presence of the apostles.
   b. We can imitate this example by making time in our own busy days for prayer.

3. Jesus gives us a glimpse of the final judgment, when the sheep will be separated from the goats. If we want to be like the sheep, then we need to develop family activities like the ones Jesus mentions: feeding the hungry at a homeless shelter, collecting clothing for the less fortunate, giving food on a regular basis to the local food bank, caring for the sick and elderly, or visiting those in nursing homes and prisons.

4. This verse encourages us to show hospitality to strangers, "for thereby some have entertained angels unawares."

Chapter 10

1. In evangelization, it's important to foster love and unity among all Christians, to be tenderhearted and humble, to be prepared for the questions of others, to discuss the faith with gentleness and reverence, and to return good for evil.

2. We need to live our faith well. We can be hospitable and good Christians in all our thoughts, words and deeds, always living the beatitudes of Christ.

3. Abraham was chosen by God to receive blessings so that he and his children might obey God's commands.

4. Our families can evangelize all people by our witness to Christ. We can look for opportunities to share our faith and live our Christianity well.

5. First, be sure to pass on your faith to your children. Then, look for opportunities to share the Gospel with your neighbors. Finally, develop a plan to help lead other persons or groups to Christ, and evaluate this plan yearly. Some families may wish to write out their objectives or goals for evangelization.

6. Paul shared both the Gospel and his very life and self with the people.

7. Saints Paul and Timothy show us that sincere friendship and encouragement are very important in imitating Christ's charity and zeal for souls.

8. It is important to remember that others look to us for mentoring and encouragement. By our words and deeds, we can be a good example to our friends; otherwise, our faith might be discredited. Non-Christians are going to be especially critical of how we live day by day. Our lives may be the only

witness that touches their heart. The way we talk, act, and think needs to be sincere and Christian to its core in order for us to be effective witnesses in the world. If we give a bad example, non-Christians may have something "evil to say of us" and not be attracted to Christ and His Church.

Additional Resources

This section lists additional resources for Bible study leaders and anyone else interested in further study. Most of these books and other resources are available from Benedictus Books [(888) 316-2640].

In addition to the Bible and the Catechism, there are five papal documents that form an almost irreplaceable foundation for a study of marriage and family life:

- Pope Leo XIII, Encyclical Letter on Christian Marriage *Arcanum* (February 10, 1880)
- Pope Pius XI, Encyclical Letter on Christian Marriage *Casti Connubii* (December 31, 1930)
- Pope Paul VI, Encyclical Letter on the Regulation of Birth *Humanae Vitae* (July 25, 1968)
- Pope John Paul II, Apostolic Exhortation on the Role of the Christian Family in the Modern World *Familiaris Consortio* (November 22, 1981)
- Pope John Paul II, Letter to Families *Gratissimam Sane* (February 2, 1994)

Suggested Magazines

We highly recommend these three magazines:

- *Faith & Family: The Magazine of Catholic Living*, P.O. Box 369, Mt. Morris, IL 61054-0369; (800) 421-3230
- *Catholic Parent*, Our Sunday Visitor, 200 Noll Plaza, Huntington, IN 46750; (800) 348-2440
- *Lay Witness*, Catholics United for the Faith, 827 N. Fourth St., Steubenville, OH 43952; (800) MY-FAITH.

Chapter 1

Catechism (nos. 1, 1996-2005, 2010)

Chapter 2

The Catechism has a wonderful section devoted to the Sacrament of Marriage (nos. 1601-66). We don't have the space to quote it all, so we encourage you to take some time to read the passage slowly and savor its rich teaching.

There are some profound insights in Pope John Paul II's *Familiaris Consortio* and Pope Paul VI's *Humanae Vitae*, which we encourage couples to read together and discuss. We make special note of only a few paragraphs (*Familiaris Consortio*, nos. 13, 19, 56; *Humanae Vitae*, no. 9), but don't allow our limited citations to hold you back if you want to read the documents in their entirety.

Oscar and Susan Staudt's *Creative Abstinence* (Cincinnati: Couple to Couple League, 1999) is another helpful resource. To order this pamphlet, contact the Couple to Couple League [P.O. Box 111184, Cincinnati, OH 45211-1184; (800) 745-8252].

Chapter 3

The Two Sides of Love (Colorado Springs: Focus on the Family, 1992) and *Love Is a Decision: Proven Techniques to Keep Your Marriage Alive and Lively* (Dallas: Word, 1989), both by Gary Smalley and John Trent, are exceptional reading for developing a stronger marriage through communication.

We recommend three other resources:

- Proverbs 31 (for wives)
- Tim Gray and Curtis Martin, *Boys to Men:*
  The Transforming Power of Virtue
  (Steubenville: Emmaus Road Publishing, 2001)
- Rev. Lawrence Lovasik, *The Hidden Power of Kindness*
  (Manchester, N.H.: Sophia Institute Press, 1999)

Chapter 4

For further reading about the relationship between husbands and wives, we recommend three papal documents:

- Pope Pius XI, *Casti Connubii*
- Pope John Paul II, *Familiaris Consortio*
- Pope John Paul II, Apostolic Letter on the Dignity and
  Vocation of Women *Mulieris Dignitatem* (August 15, 1988)

Chapter 5

We highly recommend to couples who wish to reflect further on marital intimacy the entire Song of Solomon and *The Two Sides of Love* by Garry Smalley and John Trent.

Chapter 6

For additional reading on openess to life, we recommend the following resources:

- Catechism (nos. 2360-2400, on marital love)
- Second Vatican Council, Pastoral Constitution on the Church in the Modern World *Gaudium et Spes* (December 7, 1965), nos. 50-51
- Pope Paul VI, *Humanae Vitae*, nos. 11-16
- Kimberly Hahn, *Life-Giving Love: Embracing God's Beautiful Design for Marriage* (Ann Arbor, Mich.: Servant Publications, 2002)

For information about responsible parenthood, we recommend contacting the following organizations:

- Couple to Couple League [(513) 471-2000; http://www.ccli.org]
- Billings Ovulation Method [P.O. Box 16206, St. Paul, MN 55116; (651) 699-8139; http://www.billingsmethod.com]
- Pope Paul VI Institute [6901 Mercy Rd., Omaha, NE, 68106; (402) 390-9167; http://www.popepaulvi.com]

Chapter 7

The following six works have assisted us in our desire to form godly children:

- Ephesians 4:31-32 (if you battle with a hot temper)
- Catechism, nos. 2197-2257 (on the Fourth Commandment)
- Sophia Cavalletti, *The Religious Potential of the Child* (New York: Paulist Press, 1983)
- David Isaacs, *Character Building* (Portland, Oreg.: Four Courts Press, 2001)
- Michael O'Brien, *A Landscape with Dragons* (San Francisco: Ignatius Press, 1998)
- Rev. Jesus Urtega, *God and Children* (Chicago: Scepter, 1964)

Chapter 8

We recommend five resources to those who wish to reflect further upon the financial principles discussed in chapter 8:

- Ron Blue, *Master Your Money* (Nashville: Thomas Nelson Publishers, 1997)
- Ron Blue, *Mastering Money in Your Marriage: Personal Study Guide* (Ventura, Calif.: Gospel Light, 1997)
- Larry Burkett, *The Complete Financial Guide for Young Couples* (Wheaton, Ill.: Victor Books, 1989)
- Larry Burkett, *Debt-Free Living* (Chicago: Moody Press, 1989)
- Philip Lenahan, *Finances for Today's Catholic Family* (Temecula, Calif.: Financial Foundations for the Family, 1996)

Chapter 9
These three resources can help you create a Catholic culture of prayer in your home:

- Catechism (nos. 1113-34, on the sacraments; nos. 2201-57, on the family in God's plan; nos. 2697-2745, on the life of prayer; and nos. 2683-96, on guides to prayer)
- Michaelann Martin, Carol Puccio, and Zoë Romanowsky, *The Catholic Parent Book of Feasts* (Huntington, Ind.: Our Sunday Visitor, 1999)
- Rev. Peter-Thomas Rohrbach, *Conversation with Christ: An Introduction to Mental Prayer* (Chicago: Fides Publishers, 1956)

Chapter 10
These two books will help you put into practice your family's mission to evangelize, beginning with your own home:

- Rev. Lawrence Lovasik, *The Catholic Family Handbook: Time Tested Techniques to Help You Strengthen Your Marriage and Raise Good Kids* (Manchester, N.H.: Sophia Institute Press, 2001)
- John Trent, Rick Osborne, and Kurt Bruner, eds., *Parents' Guide to the Spiritual Growth of Children: Helping Your Child Develop a Personal Faith* (Colorado Springs: Focus on the Family, 2000)

The following organizations can also strengthen your family life:

- Apostolate for Family Consecration [3375 Rt. 36, Bloomingdale, OH 43910; (800) FOR-MARY; http://www.familyland.org]
- FAMILIA (Family Life in America) [Legionaries of Christ, 475 Oak Ave., Cheshire, CT 06410; (203) 271-0805; http://www.legionofchrist.org]

- Forming Families [P.O. Box 95, Littleton, CO 80160; (303) 703-9603]
- National Cursillo Center [P.O. Box 210226, Dallas, TX 75211; (214) 339-6321; http://www.natl-cursillo.org]
- Retrouvaille (for spouses who are facing difficulties in their marriage) [http://www.retrouvaille.org]
- St. Joseph's Covenant Keepers [22226 Westchester Blvd., Port Charlotte, FL 33952; (941) 764-7725; http://www.dads.org]
- Teams of Our Lady [P.O. Box 1058, Vienna, VA 22183; (703) 281-4816; http://www.teamsofourlady.org]
- Worldwide Marriage Encounter [2210 E. Highland Ave., Suite 106, San Bernardino, CA 92404; (909) 863-9963; http://www.wwme.org]